DISCARD

the calcutta kitchen   রান্নাবান্না, কলকাতার খাবার

the calcutta kitchen

Simon Parkes &
Udit Sarkhel

Interlink Books

An imprint of Interlink Publishing Group, Inc.
Northampton, Massachusetts

First American edition published in 2007 by

INTERLINK BOOKS
An imprint of Interlink Publishing Group, Inc.
46 Crosby Street, Northampton, Massachusetts 01060
www.interlinkbooks.com

ISBN-10: 1-56656- 671-1 (hardback)

ISBN-13: 978-1-56656- 671-1 (hardback)

While all reasonable care has been taken during the
preparation of this edition, neither the publisher, editors,
nor the authors can accept responsibility for any
consequences arising from the use thereof or from the
information contained therein.

Recipe introductions and recipes plus *The Bengali Kitchen*
written by Udit Sarkhel, main book introduction and
chapter introductions by Simon Parkes.

Printed and bound in China

To request our complete 40-page full-color catalog,
please call us toll free at 1-800-238-LINK, visit our website at
www.interlinkbooks.com or write to
Interlink Publishing
46 Crosby Street, Northampton, MA 01060

For Edna Parkes and in memory of the late Stanley Parkes.

Simon Parkes

For my mum and dad — thanks for putting me on the map.

Udit Sarkhel

INTRODUCTION

The first time I went to Calcutta in the early 1990s, I took a taxi from my hotel to Mandeville Gardens in the smart suburb of Ballygunge. The driver of the battered black and yellow Ambassador cab pulled up underneath the building, and I was taken in the elevator to the eighth floor, to the apartment of R.P. Gupta. All roads, it seemed, led to R.P. I was confronted by an unstoppable, eccentric figure clad in crumpled *kurta* pajamas. His conversation ricocheted off the walls, subjects bubbling to the surface, then swiftly overtaken by others: favorite fish preparations, the perils of Calcutta's society hostesses, the joys of the mango season, reminiscences about his friend, the filmmaker Satyajit Ray.

R.P. was re-reading *Don Quixote* with relish. He could recall great European cathedral cities he had visited with his wife, Moni, and remembered being astonished by "the tintinnabulation of the bells." Once, he'd eaten at Le Grand Véfour in Paris, and he could recite the dishes he'd chosen without hesitation. The year before R.P. died, in reply to a postcard I'd sent from Liguria in Italy, he asked whether I'd visited Rapallo and Max Beerbohm's house. This former public-relations-executive-turned-writer-and-chronicler had written a book about Bengalis and fish, he was an expert on *kalighat* (temple) painting, and he would always throw out juicy tidbits — gossip, recherché facts, and useful contacts. Once, he packed me off to the confection factory of K.C. Das (who make the famous, oft-exported *rosogolla*), and another time he arranged for me to tour Gariahat Fish Market. He couldn't accompany me, so he sent along Biswanath, the building's elevator operator.

In his essay *Mercy*, the writer Colm Toibin described Satyajit Ray and the Nobel Prize-winning writer and poet Rabindranath Tagore as having "an equal sense of ownership of their own culture and that of Britain." So did R.P. He was at home in the world and possessed the ability to switch from one culture to another with consummate ease. On top of that, he never lost his curiosity about anything. Such characteristics were particular not just to him or to the two intellectual greats of 20th-century Bengali civilization; they are common to many Bengalis, who seem able to flit effortlessly between their own world and other ones that may have been visited, glimpsed through images, or, as is more likely, absorbed through words.

Once, a good friend told me, "What you've got to remember about us Bengalis is that we're only really interested in three things: educating our children, reading books and food." And in some ways, that's it in a nutshell. Here, there's a distinct attitude to food — in terms of the pleasures of the table, the authenticity of the spicing, the freshness of ingredients and the social distinctions that are brought into play. Calcuttans know and adore fish, vegetables, and sweets in particular. They revel in the subtlety of the flavors that have been built up over centuries with diligence and precision. Like Italians, they discuss meals eaten and meals yet to be eaten with relish. New and sometimes unfamiliar recipes are noted and filed away. The latest restaurants warrant endless debate. There is, quite simply, an inquisitiveness that never fades. "So, this Fat Duck outside London: tell me...?" someone once asked.

I have gone back to Calcutta many times since that first visit and lived there for more than a year, starting in 1999. Invariably I fly in and, if it's during daylight hours, the first thing I see as the plane drops below the cloud line is the glint of light on an endless matrix of ponds, water tanks, and rivers, as well as the great, snaking river Hoogly (distributary of the symbolic and mighty river Ganges). Apart from the intermittent dotting of buildings, I see a bed of green made up of coconut palms, banana trees, rice paddies, and lush vegetation, regardless of the time of year. And I remember that the plane possibly began its descent way before dipping below the Tropic of Cancer. This is the fertile hinterland that shapes and provides

Gourmet and purveyor of exotic Bengali tidbits, R.P. Gupta. (Photograph by Simon Parkes)

for the metropolis I now consider a home. I came to realize, many years ago, that for all its faults and difficulties, Calcutta — for me — is some sort of still point in the turning world.

Little can prepare you for that first onslaught: the sheer weight of population, the noise, the twisted symphony of car horns and crows, the belching smoke of bus and lorry exhausts, the utter mishmash of everything. Every surface is scrawled or written upon: political slogans, the constant putting up and tearing down of film posters, indiscriminate advertising, and news on the latest ringtones just waiting to be downloaded. There are people on bicycles and rickshaws and people on motorbikes wearing funny helmets, with elegant women riding on the back in cool-colored saris. Entire divisions of bright-yellow Ambassador taxis circle endlessly like shoals of fish.

The heat, the humidity, and the rains age things rapidly: it's hard trying to decipher what's old and what's not, especially in a city where nothing's been around for more than 300 years. After all, Job Charnock, the East India Company's chief agent in the Hoogly area, only dropped anchor on a sultry monsoon afternoon in August 1690. Before he bowled up, there were just three villages: Sutanuti, Govindapur, and Kalikata. As you stagger into the first of many traffic jams, it's easy to agree with those who've described it as the parvenu city, a haphazardly planned upstart. It was Rudyard Kipling who said Calcutta was "chance-directed, chance-erected." Through its imperial gates, you might glimpse the colonnaded facade of the Raj Bhavan (formerly Government House), with its architectural nod to Kedlestone Hall in Derbyshire, or see other increasingly rare buildings with classical proportions

and ornamentation that hint of another, less chaotic era, one now long gone.

And, one day, you might visit the emblematic Victoria Memorial, with its Raj relics, its grand statues and portraits and its museum outlining the history of the city. In one corner, there's a quote I've often reflected upon that says, "No other Indian city benefited in quite the same way from British rule, but no other city had to pay as high a price, either." And that high price is markedly visible. Since Partition, wave after wave of refugees from the former East Bengal (now Bangladesh) have washed up on Calcutta, and nowhere is it possible to completely escape the privations of the poor. Lives are lived out in public places: people wash, do their laundry, and clean their teeth at the water hydrants; they make shelters, sleep, cook, play, argue, and love as others pass by. Here, in a city where estimates put the population at at least 14 million, such things are unavoidable. And while the poverty and squalor sometimes hits you right between the eyes and transfixes you, there is also animation, humor, and dignity.

If one of the benchmarks of a great city is the range and diversity of its culinary culture, then Calcutta's place in the overall scheme of things is assured. What is clear is that certain dishes tell you much about a slice of the city's history and evolution. Legend has it that the favorite meal during the Bengali monsoon, *khichuri* (a meal of rice and dal which, many variants later, ended up in the anglicized form as kedgeree), was served to Job Charnock after his trip downriver to Sutanuti.

Before the British arrived, it was the Portuguese who introduced papaya, cashew nut, tomato, and, most importantly, chili to the diet. By way of Goa

(which remained a Portuguese colony until 1961), we get vindaloo, traditionally made from pork using good wine vinegar. The city's fascination with the mango was established by the Muslim Nawabs of Murshidabad, who propagated new fragrant varieties in the orchards of North Bengal. Moghul rulers also brought the *pulao* and the biryani to the table, as well as the velvety-smooth sophisticated *shami* kebabs and the more prosaic *kathi* roll, the ultimate fast-food delicacy.

In the early days of the British in Calcutta, the wealthy merchants (or nabobs) led lives and ate food heavily influenced by local custom. As British power grew, so did British tastes and diets. Curries and rice gave way to soups, roasts, and puddings. Tucked away in the memsahib's kitchen, her cook produced hybrid dishes such as *countree koptan* or, to give it its more recognizable title, chicken "country captain." Calcutta is also home to the oldest China Town outside China, producing Hakka and Cantonese cooking and spawning a huge network of eateries, both cheap and smart, across town. Refugees who have found their way here have all left their gastronomic mark: the Burmese *khow suey*, Tibetan *momos*, Armenian *dolmas,* and the Jewish *aloo makallah.*

Then, of course, there's Bengali cooking, although until recently, it was almost impossible to taste it unless you were invited to a private home. What a pity! True, it can be labor-intensive and, as family networks change, the passing on of skills from one generation to the next rarely happens. Nonetheless, this is some of the most sophisticated cooking in India and possesses a subtle range of flavors and tastes enhanced by careful spicing.

In this global age, it is a paradox that we seek out cooking that is regional and authentic. Yet, what largely passes off as Indian food in Britain is mainly rich north Indian food cooked by Bangladeshis, often with spices crushed and mixed as if with a sledge-hammer. Bengali food could make many of us rethink our ideas about food from the subcontinent. It's a cuisine with haute aspirations, with its inexhaustible roll-call of fishes and vegetables, its pungency derived from the widespread use of mustard (seeds and oil), its tempering with a blend of five spices called panch phoran, and the clear order in which dishes are consumed.

Calcuttans have never been very good at promoting themselves and always seem to be at the mercy of events. It's as if somewhere deep in the bowels of the political heart of the city there is a public-relations machine cranked permanently into reverse gear. The Black Hole, economic collapse, the Bengali famine of 1943, and Mother Teresa's work with the sick all shape — and spring from — the image of the city we keep in our popular sub-conscious. The intellectual rigor and flirtations of people like R.P. Gupta, the cultural awareness of the broad sweep of the population, and the rich culinary strands of the city square less easily with that view.

In this book, we go to fish ponds and markets, artisan food producers (although such an expression would be unheard of), restaurants, and clubs; we hear the recollections of cooks and gourmets, and we are dazzled by the freshness of what is cooked on the street. We make no claims to have touched upon every aspect of Calcutta's food story. This isn't an exhaustive examination and set of recipes; merely a series of snapshots — but ones taken with love.

— Simon Parkes

কলকাতার রান্নাঘর

THE BENGALI
KITCHEN

I am Bengali, so I'm going to tell you a bit about Bengal. It is one of the eastern states of India, where the river Ganges, in the guise of the river Hoogly, meets the Bay of Bengal. Calcutta, the city of the goddess Kali, is the capital and the nerve center of Bengal. This state is politically important in India, and commercially controls the jute, tea, and most of the rice markets for the whole country. There are also excellent silks from Murshidabad and terra cotta from Bankura. Bengalis are well respected by all Indians as sentimentalists, with a love for literature, art, theater and food. They are famous for their oratorical skills, and poetry seems to be a natural part of life, so it is not surprising that Bengal has produced some of the world's greatest poets, such as Tagore and Nazrul Islam. It could be said that each Bengali lives his or her life as if it were a drama in a Satyajit Ray film.

The Bengali style of cooking is one of the most sophisticated in India. Like other cuisines in the subcontinent, it was influenced by the Ayurveda, an ancient Hindu treatise on health dating from 1500 BC. The philosophy of Ayurveda is a healthy maintenance of mind, body, and soul. Food being the fuel of life, many Ayurvedic references were recipe- and ingredient-linked. Herbs and spices, which are probably used more in India's cooking than in any other national cuisine, were and are included for medicinal purposes as well as for flavoring. Turmeric, for instance, is widely used as a yellow colorant, but it is also believed to be antiseptic — which is why the ground spice is often rubbed into raw fish before cooking.

The Bengali cuisine has also, like the rest of the country, been influenced by many foreign cuisines as a result of invasion, rule by invaders, settlers, and migrants from neighboring countries. The Moghuls or Mongols brought the influence of their great empire (which encompassed Afghanistan, much of Persia, and the north of the Indian subcontinent) in the seventh century. Many familiar Indian dishes, such as *pulao* (*polo* or *pilaf*), biryani, kebabs, and kormas originate from Persia.

The 200 years of British rule during the Raj were of minor importance gastronomically, but they did increase a European awareness of spicy food, making curry (from the South Indian word *kari*) a household name. Since then, many others have come to India, and Bengal in particular, including the Armenians, Jews (many from Iraq), Chinese, and Tibetans. All of them have contributed to formulating the Bengali kitchen.

Religion has also played a huge part in establishing the cuisines of India, including that of Bengal. Jains, a Hindu sect, and many other Hindus in the south of the country are vegetarian; meat-eating Hindus revere the cow, and so do not eat beef. The Moghuls were Muslim, and present-day Muslims do not eat pork. The Persian Zoroastrians, fleeing Muslim rule in the eighth century, became known as Parsees (Persians), and they, too, introduced unique Persian touches. Christianity was known in India before the 16th century, but it was the arrival of the Portuguese at that time that was hugely significant: they brought the chili pepper for a start (itself newly introduced to Europe from South America) and a new sort of heat to subcontinental cooking (heat was previously supplied by mustard seeds, ginger, and black pepper).

With all these strands to the cuisine, the Bengali kitchen remains unique. Rice is the staple, much more so than wheat (which was introduced fairly recently after rationing in the 1960s during the border war between India and China). Legumes are vital, and hardly a day goes by without a Bengali eating some form of dal (which can be made of lentils, whole or split peas, or beans). Many legume and rice dishes play a large part in religious and other feasts.

Fresh vegetables and fruit are primary ingredients of most meals, and a typical Bengali family will shop daily for them; no shopping spree is complete without some friendly bartering for even the smallest amounts. Fish is the main protein, as Bengalis are inveterate eaters of fish, and no good meal would be complete without fish or shrimp. The fish are freshwater or sweetwater rather than from the sea, as Bengal does not have easy access to the seafood-rich Bay of Bengal. The fish come instead mainly from the vast networks of rivers and ponds. Meat plays a less important part in the Bengali kitchen: as pork and beef are proscribed for many, lamb, goat and, increasingly, poultry, are the main choices, but fish is still much more important and appreciated.

Spicing in Bengal differs from that in other parts of India. Mustard is used as greens, as ground seeds, and as a pungent, pure oil that is the principal cooking medium (apart from ghee, a clarified butter often made from buffalo milk). Ginger, cumin, and chili are the other spice mainstays; garlic is more a flavoring of the cooking of East Bengal (now Bangladesh), than of West Bengal and Calcutta. If not strictly speaking a spice, sugar is used a lot in savory cooking in West Bengal, and this again clearly distinguishes between the food of West and East. Spice combinations are important, primarily garam masala (see page 21) and panch phoran (see page 54). All spices are ground fresh daily; this would be done in most households by the kitchen help, while the all-important combining of the spices for specific dishes would be done by the cook or the housewife herself.

I cannot conclude my introduction to the Bengalis and their cooking without disclosing their compulsive love of sweets and "anytime" snacking. Bengal's great contribution to food is its variety of sweets made from reduced milk, curdled milk, and split milk. They form an endless procession in a rainbow of colors with different textures, often with one type stuffed inside another. Bengalis eat sweets at any time of the day: mid-morning, mid-afternoon with tea, when visitors come, after a meal, and on family occasions. Bengal is also renowned for its variety of "chops" (croquettes), which are savory vegetarian fried snacks. As a sign of hospitality to any visitor, no matter how casual the visit is, Bengalis offer tea, *sandesh* (a sweet made from curdled milk), and *shingaras* (which are first cousins of the better-known samosas).

Having said all this about the importance of food in the Bengali lifestyle: the first loves of Bengalis are, and always will be, intelligent reading, music, and theater.

—Udit Sarkhel

বাঙালী বাড়ির রান্না

BENGALI
HOME COOKING

Pieces of boal fish, cooked in turmeric, red chilli paste, onions and garlic, lay in a red fiery sauce in a flat pan; rice, packed into an even white cake, had a spade-like spoon embedded in it; slices of fried aubergine were arranged on a white dish; dal was served from another pan with a drooping ladle; long, complex filaments of banana-flower, exotic, botanical, lay in yet another pan in a dark sauce; each plate had a heap of salt on one side, a green chilli, and a slice of sweet-smelling lemon. The grown-ups snapped the chillies (each made a sound terse as a satirical retort), and scattered the tiny, deadly seeds in their food. If any of the boys were ever brave or foolish enough to bite a chilli, their eyes filled tragically with tears, and they longed to drown in a cool, clear lake. Though Chhotomama was far from affluent, they ate well, especially on Sundays, caressing the rice and the sauces on their plates with attentive, sensuous fingers, fingers which performed a practised and graceful ballet on the plate till it was quite empty.

Amit Chaudhuri, *A Strange and Sublime Address* (Pan Macmillan, 1992)

Much has been made of the polarization of life in India, where rich rubs up against poor and rural rubs up against urban. Yet Calcutta seems to be shaped by the manners, restraint, and high-mindedness of the Bengali middle classes.

The more bourgeois layers of the Bengali class system are known as the *bhadralok*. While I've no idea whether a fictional character such as Chhotomama (mentioned in the quote above; a family appellation meaning youngest maternal uncle) slots in here or not, I bet he'd be the type to go off early on a Sunday morning to do what is quaintly referred to as "the marketing," especially for fish. This is not to be entrusted to his wife or a servant.

Financial stringency may mean Chhotomama doesn't have the wherewithal to do up his house. But he'll haggle with the vendor and bring back a plump *hilsa* fish crammed full of eggs. He'll describe his wife's *mocha* recipe to his work colleagues as though it were an ornate sunset. It's true he's on his uppers, but he can afford good food, and probably a music

teacher to give his daughter private tuition — and each year he'll go to the Calcutta Book Fair in January and lineup for tickets for the Visconti season at Nandan film theater. He's a welter of contradictions. By nature he's conservative, though he might well vote Communist in the state elections (West Bengal has had a Communist-led Left Front government for over 25 years). He may lament Calcutta's decline and remember a time when the city's fire hydrants were polished and the streets hosed down twice a day. Over this decay he has no control. However, over the purchase of key ingredients he is his own master.

Of the year I lived in Calcutta, one evening stands out. I was invited to the home of Mr. and Mrs. Sinha (his family were formerly the Rajas of Paikpara and probably hovered above the level of *bhadralok*). A car was dispatched to collect me — the driver's jacket and gloves matched the clinical white seat covers — and take me to a big detached house on Sarat Bose Road (formerly Lansdowne Road).

I wrote in my diary the next day, "50 years of Independence may have changed the names, but not the degree of affluence and worldliness." A small team of servers brought drinks and snacks and hovered behind the 10 of us having dinner around a circular table rich with frangipani blossoms and family silver. Apart from the civilized, intoxicating atmosphere, what stood out was the regimented way in which the dishes came and went. With the exception of the constant presence of rice and endless trays of feather-light *luchis*, everything was clearly delineated and ordered. This is the Bengali way.

Here, as opposed to elsewhere in India, dishes are eaten separately before the next one is commenced (in marked contrast to, say, the Punjab, where people freely mix what is on the table). Meals are served on a *thala*, or plate of bell-metal or terra cotta lined with banana leaf, with a series of small bowls arranged around the outside like orbiting planets. On the plate are rice and a trinity of salt, lime wedge, and green chili. Ghee is served first, followed by the contents of the first side dish, a *shukto* or bitter vegetable preparation. Then comes dal, followed by other vegetable and potato items. After that, fish prepared with the mildest spices and gravies first, and fuller fish dishes next. Then chicken or mutton if there's any meat, followed by chutney with fried *papar* (poppadums). To round things off, a sweet milk-based dessert such as *mishti doi* or sweetened yogurt.

Why this order? I'm sure ancient texts have hinted at auspicious and balanced links between food, character, and well-being. But there is a natural progression of tastes to this way of eating, taking in bitter, astringent, sour, salty, and pungent, and winding up with sweet. Simple tastes are established before complex ones, light before rich ones.

Food here remains locked into a seasonal cycle and ingredients are measured in terms of their health, as well as culinary, value. The aesthetics of food — colors, textures, shapes, the interplay of certain spices — are paramount. I remember being baffled (and ill-prepared) the first time I ate nutty-tasting dal, carp smeared with mustard, shrimp with pumpkin, bitter-tasting gourds, and so on. Such things were light-years away from anything that purported to be Indian food served in England. Here were complex and haunting flavors on one hand, yet with none of the overbearing fiery richness and oiliness so often associated with food from the subcontinent.

Few people sit surrounded by such an elegant backdrop as the Sinha house — but many eat as well, if not as lavishly. I have no idea who cooked the meal of that oft-remembered evening, but I have seen and watched the methods of many others who create so much from so little. The Bengali kitchen is low on accessories and paraphernalia. Here, the purpose is solely to cook. Curved metal pots and woks (the *handi* and the *karai*) get lifted on and off a compact, two-burner stove fired by bottled gas, using tongs that look like pliers. There'll be a rectangular stone for grinding spices, an upright *bonti* (blade), some spatulas, and not much more. Oh, maybe a pressure cooker, a small blender for making masalas 21st-century style, and an Aquaguard water-filter box over the sink. And rarely, but increasingly, a microwave. Fridges, to my amusement, lurk in the corners of living or dining rooms rather than kitchens.

While I was in Calcutta, my cook and server Ashok Das came to work for me. He was 17, and not long off the train from Baleswar, speaking little English. But he had a recipe book and a Bengali-Oriya-English pictorial dictionary. People told me, "He's from Orissa, and they make the best cooks." How right they were! He blended his own masalas and seasoned things to perfection. After he'd been with me for six weeks, I invited people to dinner. Ashok made a simple menu of chicken curry, rice, okra, and salad followed by caramel custard and mango salad. I'll

Moyna Jahla (far right), friend of both authors, entertaining friends with the help of her servers.

never forget the way he decorated the rice with alternating single cilantro leaves and diamond wedges of tomato. Is that what they do in Baleswar? I think not.

Years earlier, the Mogs, rather than the Oriyas, were prized. The Mogs were from a tribe in the Chittagong hill tracts and, I was told, cooked like a dream and drank like fishes. My friends Mr. and Mrs. Mukherjee reflected on their ancestral house on Lower Circular Road, where there were two kitchens. One was headed up by an Oriya *thakur* (cook) who was a Brahmin — he always did a Bengali lunch and then cooked for all the servants. At night food came from the other kitchen, where a Bengali-Christian cooked Continental Western food, including soups, grilled fish, roasts, trifle, and a savory dish. No wonder there's this easy knack for straddling two cultures.

"Our lives, like the walls of our houses, are more porous than yours," I was told by a Bengali friend once, as a woman (unknown to him) silently walked past an open doorway in his house. She'd been newly hired to do basic kitchen preparation. People float into and out of houses in Calcutta in a way that would be unthinkable in the West. The sahib and memsahib provide food and shelter and pay for servants' medical and educational needs. It's part of the deal. For the very poor, with no such safety net, I've watched as leftover rice is put in

water to be soaked. The next day, the rice and water (*panta bhat*) are eaten with oil, chili, and salt. Maybe later in the day a small fish and lentils will be bought. And life will go on.

Religion, caste, class, background, and geography all help shape and delineate the diet. As an outsider, dissecting these sub-groups is almost impossible. Are they Brahmins? Are they from East Bengal (called colloquially Bangals) or are they Ghotis from West Bengal? As Chitrita Banerji says in her essay *Of Food, Prejudice and Discovery*, "Food, cooking styles, and eating habits of rival communities were the most common mediums for couching insults, jocular or vicious."

The emphasis on what type of fish, the use of onion and garlic or poppy seeds, the eating of chapattis at dinner: all these vary and fluctuate. But more unites than divides. For an Italian, perfect pasta with a simple tomato sauce cuts a swathe across the social divide. So too in Calcutta with a dish such as *maacher jhol*. An educated *bhadralok* could easily eat from his or her servant's plate safe in the knowledge that not only is the food tasty and fresh, but it also marks shared ingredients and a shared geography. Here, there is no unswerving food industry sapping people of their family know-how, there's just a flick of the wrist as the *karai* is removed from the heat.

Chitta Ranjan, father of author Udit Sarkhel, eating Bengali food in the traditional way, which allows him to feel its texture before he enjoys its flavor.

Murgir malai curry
Mild chicken curry with coconut milk

A *malai* curry is one of the most flavorsome and delicate of tender chicken and coconut curries, something for the whole family to enjoy. Classically it is made with shrimp, and even the shells might be used. Chicken has been introduced to Bengali households only recently, over the last few decades, and cooks at home find this curry a very suitable way of cooking it.

Serves 4

3lb 8oz chicken, or the same weight of boneless chicken pieces

½ tsp salt, plus extra as needed

3 tsp turmeric

juice of 1 lemon

3 medium onions, peeled and roughly chopped

6 garlic cloves, peeled and roughly chopped

1-inch piece fresh ginger, peeled and roughly chopped

1 tsp cumin seeds

2 tsp brown mustard seeds

⅞ cup coconut milk

2 tbsp mustard oil

1 bay leaf

½ tsp red chili powder

3 medium fresh green chilis, finely chopped

1 cup creamed coconut

½ tsp sugar

3 sprigs fresh cilantro, torn into pieces

1 Skin, bone, and wash the chicken, then cut it into 16 even-size pieces. Put the pieces in a dish. Mix ½ tsp of the salt with 1 tsp of the turmeric and the lemon juice, and rub this into the chicken. Set aside.

2 Put the onion, garlic, ginger, cumin seeds, and mustard seeds into a blender and process to a thick paste. If this is too dry, add a little of the coconut milk to thin it.

3 Heat the mustard oil in a deep saucepan with a lid over medium heat. Add the bay leaf, red chili powder, and the onion paste, and fry for 10–12 minutes, stirring continuously. You may need to add a little water. Add the chicken pieces, the remaining turmeric, and the green chilis and stir well. Cover and cook for another 10 minutes, checking and stirring occasionally. The chicken should be almost cooked.

4 Add the creamed coconut and the coconut milk, and mix well. Simmer for 3–4 minutes, until the chicken is cooked through, add the sugar, and season with salt if needed. The sauce should not be runny. Serve with boiled rice, sprinkled with the fresh cilantro.

Pathar jhol
Goat meat curry

Bengalis cook and eat both male and female goats. The male is castrated and fattened up, therefore the meat is fattier. The female is leaner, and that is what would be used here — *pathar*. Buy goat meat from a good Asian or Afro-Caribbean butcher; it is sold cubed on the bone. It's worth checking that there are no sharp bone chips due to incorrect cutting.

Serves 4

1lb 12oz goat meat on the bone, cubed

2 tsp salt, plus extra as needed

3 tbsp mustard oil

1 tbsp red chili powder (more if you like it hot)

3 tsp turmeric

5 medium fresh green chilis

2 dried bay leaves

8 garlic cloves, peeled and finely chopped

1-inch piece fresh ginger, peeled and chopped

1¼ cups hot water

1 tsp sugar

3 medium onions, peeled and finely chopped

2 tsp ground cumin

3 tbsp ground coriander

5 medium tomatoes, chopped

1 tbsp malt vinegar

2 tsp garam masala

Garam masala

10 1-inch cinnamon sticks

25 green cardamom pods

10 cloves

5 medium dried bay leaves

1 Wash the cubed meat and put it in a large bowl. Rub with 2 tsp of the salt, 1 tbsp of the mustard oil, the chili powder, and 1 tsp of the turmeric. Add the chilis and bay leaves, and leave for about 15–20 minutes.

2 Preheat the oven to 375°F.

3 Blend the garlic and ginger to a smooth paste in a blender, adding about 1–1½ tbsp of the water.

4 In a heavy-bottomed casserole dish with a lid, heat the remaining mustard oil on the stovetop over medium heat. Add the sugar and fry until it just starts turning color. Add the onion and fry for a few minutes until light brown, then add the garlic-ginger paste. Fry for 2–3 minutes, until you can smell the fried garlic. Add the remaining turmeric and the cumin and coriander and fry for 2–3 minutes more.

5 Add the goat meat, and fry without adding any liquid for a good 5–6 minutes, until browning. Add the tomatoes, salt to taste, and the remaining water, and mix well. Cover and cook, checking and stirring occasionally, for 12–15 minutes, adding some more hot water if necessary.

6 After this time, add the vinegar and check the consistency of the sauce; the meat should be submerged in the liquid. Cover and cook for 20 minutes in the oven.

7 Remove the lid, and stir it once — adding a little more water if necessary — then return to the oven, cover and cook for another 20 minutes until tender.

8 To make the garam masala, lightly toast the spices and grind them in a mill to a fine powder. Cool and store in an airtight jar.

9 Sprinkle the dish with the garam masala, and eat with boiled rice or with *luchis* (*see* page 66).

Kosha mangsho
Pot-roasted lamb with spices

This method of cooking lamb is used by almost every household, for it's so easy, but it was given a special status by a small eatery in north Calcutta which, to this day, maintains its consistency in serving the dish. The dish more commonly carries the name *Golbari'r kosha mangsho*, after the restaurant.

Serves 4

1lb 12oz boneless leg of lamb, cut into 1-inch cubes

salt

2 tbsp vegetable oil

6 medium potatoes, peeled and halved

2 cups hot water

3–4 tsp garam masala (*see* page 21)

Marinade

3 tsp turmeric

2 tsp red chili powder

2 tsp ground cumin

2 tbsp ground coriander

2 bay leaves

4–6 medium fresh green chilis

3 medium onions, peeled and chopped

6–8 garlic cloves, peeled and chopped

½-inch piece fresh ginger, peeled and chopped

8 medium tomatoes, left whole

3 tbsp mustard oil

1 tsp sugar

1 Wash the lamb pieces, and mix with all the marinade ingredients in a large bowl. Add a little salt to taste. Leave for at least 2 hours to marinate (or, if kept in the fridge, up to 24 hours).

2 In a heavy-bottomed casserole dish on the stoveop, heat the vegetable oil to smoking, cool a little, and add the meat with all the marinade. Stir-fry for 12–15 minutes.

3 Preheat the oven to 375°F.

4 Add the potatoes and hot water. Stir to mix well, then season to taste. Cover and cook in the oven for 20 minutes. Remove from the oven to check the liquid level — the gravy should be just coating the meat — then return to the oven for another 10 minutes.

5 Remove from the oven, stir in the garam masala, and simmer on top of the stove until the excess liquid has evaporated, another 2–3 minutes.

6 Serve with *luchis* (*see* page 66) or *porothas* (*see* page 152).

༄ Maacher hara gouri
Wrapped parcels of fish with mustard and tamarind

The Bengali name of this dish indicates a fish with two flavors: one side of it has a sweet marinade, the other a sharp and hot one. The marinated fish is wrapped in a banana leaf, which seals in the flavors and lends its own flavor. (You can use foil instead of the leaf, as long as you grease it well.) In some houses the parcels are buried in freshly cooked rice and left for 10 minutes, infusing the rice with the leaf flavor, too. The parcels are finished off in a hot pan as below.

Serves 4

1lb 12oz skinless filet of halibut or cod

1 tsp salt

1 tbsp lemon juice

1 large banana leaf (or greased aluminum foil), cut into 5-inch squares

1 tbsp vegetable oil

Marinade 1

3 tbsp brown mustard seeds, soaked in 2 tbsp hot water

3 medium fresh green chilis

1 tsp turmeric

½ tsp salt

2 tsp mustard oil

Marinade 2

2 tbsp tamarind pulp

2 tsp grated jaggery or soft brown sugar

½ tsp red chili powder

½ tsp ground cumin

a pinch of salt

1 Wash the fish and cut it into 8 pieces. Rub in the 1 tsp of the salt and the lemon juice, and set aside.

2 For the first marinade, put the mustard seeds and their liquid into the blender along with the fresh chilis, turmeric, and the ½ tsp salt, and process to a smooth paste. Add the mustard oil.

3 For the second marinade, mix the tamarind pulp with the jaggery (or brown sugar), red chili powder, cumin, and the pinch of salt. Mix to make a smooth paste. Place over low heat for 3–4 minutes to make sure the jaggery melts. Add a few drops of hot water if necessary. Cool before applying marinade to fish.

4 Coat one side of each piece of fish with the mustard marinade, and place on a piece of banana leaf (or foil) mustard-side down. Coat the top of the fish pieces with the tamarind marinade. Fold over the sides of the wrapper, and secure with a wooden toothpick or, better, with kitchen string. Put the parcels in a steamer, cover, and steam for about 10 minutes.

5 Heat the vegetable oil in a nonstick pan over medium heat, and arrange the steamed parcels in the pan. Fry for a minute on one side, then turn over and fry for another minute or so. This infuses the fish with the flavor of the banana leaf. If wrapping in foil, you still need to fry the parcels, as the spicy flavors are not properly released by steaming alone. Serve with boiled rice.

tip: If you heat the banana leaf pieces a little before using — in the microwave or over a flame, this will make them pliable and much easier to fold.

12 Deemer bora
Boiled egg fritters

This dish is eaten with rice and dal or kedgeree (*khichuri*). The egg fritters add an interesting crunch to an otherwise simple meal of dal and rice. The yolk can be removed and spiced up separately, then replaced in the white. You can add other ingredients to this, such as shrimp or fish flakes, to turn a simple dish into something more complex.

Serves 4

4 medium eggs, hard-boiled and shelled

1 tsp turmeric

2 tsp red chili powder

½ tsp salt

1 tbsp all-purpose flour

1 tbsp chickpea flour

3 tbsp water

⅓-inch piece fresh ginger, peeled and chopped

2 garlic cloves, peeled and chopped

vegetable oil

1 Cut the eggs in half lengthwise.

2 Combine all the other ingredients, apart from the vegetable oil, into a batter. Coat the eggs with this, and pan-fry in hot oil, taking care that the yolks stay in place in the whites.

3 Drain well, and serve with rice and dal.

Deemer aamlet curry
Masala omelet curry

Bengalis are passionate about shopping for fresh vegetables and fish every day, but sometimes – due to the rains or strikes, or even the man of the household being away – this is not possible. On an occasion like this, the *deemer* omelet curry would inevitably appear on the menu, for eggs would always be available. When I was a child, I'd look forward to days like that, as I liked the curry so much.

Serves 4

6 medium eggs

1 onion, peeled and chopped

⅓-inch piece fresh ginger, peeled and chopped

2 medium fresh green chilis, chopped

½ tsp turmeric

salt

5 sprigs fresh cilantro, 3 chopped

1 tbsp vegetable oil

Curry

2 tbsp vegetable oil

3 medium onions, peeled and chopped

2 tsp red chili powder

1 tsp turmeric

2 tsp ground cumin

2 tbsp ground coriander

6–8 medium tomatoes, chopped

2 tbsp plain yogurt

a pinch of sugar

salt

1 Break the eggs into a bowl, beat, then mix in all the remaining omelet ingredients except for the whole sprigs of cilantro and the vegetable oil.

2 Heat 1 tbsp oil in an omelet pan medium-low heat, then pour out any excess into a dish, leaving just enough to cook 1 omelet. Pour in about a third of the omelet mixture. Cook to set the bottom, then fold over from both sides; the middle of the omelet might still be a little runny. Flip over in the pan and cook for less than a minute, keeping the folded shape. Remove from the pan and keep to one side. Make 2 more omelets in the same way, greasing the pan each time with a coating of oil as above. Slice each of the folded omelets into 3–4 pieces.

3 For the curry, in an open shallow pan — a paella pan or a large frying pan — heat the 2 tbsp vegetable oil over medium heat. Fry the onion until light brown, then add all the spices. Stir for a few minutes, then add the tomatoes, and cook for about 6–8 minutes. Stir the yogurt with a fork to loosen it, then add it to the curry with the sugar and some salt to taste. Simmer for about 8–10 minutes.

4 Arrange the pieces of rolled omelet in the curry, and simmer for a couple of minutes. Sprinkle with the remaining cilantro, torn into pieces, and serve with boiled rice.

:2 Posto bata
Spiced ground poppy seeds

Posto bata is more of an accompaniment to the main meal, almost like a relish or chutney, and is not cooked (although *see* below). Very simply, it is soaked ground poppy seeds with light spicing. Poppy seeds are easily digestible in the summer heat of India. They have a light, nutty flavor, and act as a neutral medium for highlighting other tastes such as the pungency of mustard oil.

Serves 4

½ cup plus 1 tbsp poppy seeds

about ¼ tsp (or less) coarse-grained salt

1½ tbsp mustard oil

2 medium fresh green chilis, finely chopped

1 Soak the poppy seeds in barely enough water to cover for half an hour.

2 Add the salt to the seeds and water, and grind to a very fine paste, as smooth as possible. In Calcutta, they would use a grinding stone; here I find a mortar and pestle the best, which I follow with a whiz in the electric blender.

3 Add the mustard oil and chilis to the paste and mix well. Serve with rice and drier curries.

:2 Posto bata chachchari
Cooked spiced ground poppy seeds

Serves 4

1 recipe *posto bata* (*see* above)

1 tbsp vegetable oil

1 tbsp ghee

1 medium onion, peeled and finely chopped

1 tsp cumin seeds, roasted and ground

½ tsp red chili powder

salt and sugar to taste

¼ tsp garam masala (*see* page 21)

1 In a small pan, heat the oil and most of the ghee over medium heat, keeping about 1 tsp of the latter aside. Add the onion and cook for 2–3 minutes, until starting to brown. Add the cumin, red chili powder, and the *posto bata*.

2 Cook for another 3–4 minutes, then add some salt and sugar to taste. When the poppy seeds start leaving the sides of the pan easily, about 3–4 minutes, remove from heat, and mix in the reserved ghee. Sprinkle with garam masala, and serve as above.

Muri ghonto
Rice cooked with fish heads

This dish can be compared to a biryani, in that it is made with aromatic rice and fried fish, usually carp. Because of their love for fish, Bengalis do not like to waste any edible part of the fish. Fish heads are considered to be a delicacy, and are rumored to add to one's intelligence. Whenever buying and cooking fish, save the fish heads and freeze them for a future family meal, as the Bengalis do.

Serves 4

2 cups basmati rice

1 medium carp head, from a carp of about 3–4lb

1 tsp salt, plus extra as needed

3 tbsp turmeric

mustard oil

2 dried bay leaves

2 medium onions, peeled and chopped

2-inch piece fresh ginger, peeled and chopped

2 tsp ground cumin

1 tbsp ground coriander

2 tsp red chili powder

½ tsp sugar

3 medium tomatoes, chopped

2 medium potatoes, peeled and cut into ½-inch cubes

4 cups hot water

2 tsp garam masala (*see* page 21)

4 sprigs fresh cilantro, torn into pieces

1 Rinse the rice, drain it, then soak it in water to cover for about 20 minutes.

2 Preheat the oven to 350°F.

3 Split the fish head in half and remove the gills. Cut in half again lengthwise, then wash. Rub with 1 tsp each of salt and turmeric, then fry in some mustard oil over medium heat to seal and crisp on all sides, about 6–8 minutes. Drain and then set aside.

4 Strain about 2 tbsp of the mustard oil through a fine sieve into a deep casserole dish with a lid. Heat the oil to medium, add the bay leaves and onion, and fry until light brown. Add the ginger, ground spices, and remaining turmeric, and fry for a couple of minutes, then add the sugar and tomatoes, and cook for a few more minutes.

5 Drain the rice, then add it to the dish and fry for 2–3 minutes. Add the potatoes and hot water: the water should come about 1 inch above the top of the rice. Add salt to taste, and bring to a simmer. Stir, add the fish head, and cover the casserole dish.

6 Cook in the oven for about 20 minutes, until the water has been absorbed and the rice is tender. Sprinkle with the garam masala, and use a spoon to aerate the rice grains. Serve hot with the fresh cilantro sprinkled on top.

মাছ

FISH

One of my oldest friends, Biswaranjan, sings a haunting, melancholic fishermen's song from East Bengal that starts *O pio kanjan bondhu re, konba deshe jaiyo re bondhu* ("Where, my dear friend, are you going?"), and then adds that if you really are going, you should leave your *gamcha* (towel/scarf) behind with your friends — as a talisman, I suspect. I know that, as he sings, he's reminded of his ancestors who hailed from Faridpur, now part of Bangladesh. Among Calcuttans, such associations with East Bengal abound.

Nobel Prize-winning writer and poet Rabindranath Tagore came from a *zamindari* (landowning, aristocratic) family and spent many of his early years traveling to far-off estates. He was fascinated by Bengal's river network. For many people, his description of rivers, catching fish, and the darkening monsoon skies (which he referred to as the "terrible rapture") act as a touchstone to a long-gone rural past. They refer to an age, more than 100 years ago, when, as part of a wedding ceremony in East Bengal, a newly married bride first arriving at her new home would be received formally with a live *lyata* fish before releasing it into a nearby pond. Fish permeate the language. Someone with a darker side is referred to as a "deepwater fish"; someone trading on his or her innocence (as in butter wouldn't melt in the mouth) "doesn't know the proper way to eat fried fish and simply turns it over"; and someone who beats about the bush "gets the fish but not the water."

On a map, thin blue, tendril-like lines formed deep in the Himalayas travel both east from near Nepal and west from the Chinese border. As they move down through Assam or across the plains they start to converge, becoming thicker and more significant, intersecting, then branching off again, gradually making their way toward the Bay of Bengal. These lines equate to the great rivers, stamped with names that resonate, sending broad majestic sweeps and curves across the paper: the Padma, the Brahmaputra, the Meghna and, of course, the Ganges.

With these rivers comes a richness in the form of alluvial deposits and the sheer range of fish — but also, as the monsoon rains swell and burst their banks, a remorseless destructive edge. This is one of the world's largest deltaic regions and, as the rivers begin their final approach to the sea, they split and split again into a vast labyrinth of water channels and mangroves called the Sunderbans. Dotted in between are ponds and lakes: lesser territories, but ones that, for the Calcuttan, are of primary importance. The rivers, estuaries, and the sea contain saltwater fish. But it's the ponds (or tanks and bheris), with their cloudy, brackish liquid, that contain sweetwater fish. These generally smaller, bonier fish are prized above all others. Where many of them come from is astonishing.

Despite its burgeoning population, Calcutta developed along a narrow north-south axis. To the west it's hemmed in by the river Hoogly, and to the east development (until comparatively recently) was stopped by a vast area of lakes and marshland known as the Wetlands, covering some 46 square miles. Even with new roads and suburbs, the miracle is that it is largely intact. Not that many Calcuttans ever set foot in it; yet the distance from the city center to the epicenter of the Wetlands is no more than eight miles.

Mind you, getting there is hardly a joyride. Veering off the eastern bypass, past a sewerage processing plant with the deceptively palatable handle of Topsia Point A Pumping Station, you follow two canals, one perfectly normal and the other flowing slowly with fetid sludge. Gradually, you become aware of a stream of carts, trucks, and bicycles moving in the opposite direction stacked with cauliflowers or eggplants or whatever else is in season. After some miles, a series of lock-gates allow much of the bubbling, sludgy waste to be filtered off past a bizarre, abstract structure. This is the old sedimentation plant built under the British rule, but everything — filters, grit beds, and tanks — has fallen in disuse. The entire rusting Heath-Robinson enterprise is now engulfed in creeper.

This is because just over 30 years ago, a far-sighted Mr. B.N. Dutta (then chief engineer of the Calcutta Municipal Corporation) proposed a radically simpler system for pumping out both the city's sewage and excess run-off monsoon rainwater, allowing the waste to break down naturally. This is what happens today. A main distributor canal (of over 35 miles in length) weaves its way through endless lakes and *bheris*, each one separated from the other by a series of embankments. By using barriers and gates, effluent is channeled through bamboo screens, water hyacinth, and reed beds into the lakes. Bit by bit, the matter decomposes, testament to the symbiosis between bacteria and algae that not only improves water quality, but also leaves it rich in mineral deposits and plankton, making it a prime producer of some of the world's most sustainable fish.

Some 10,000 tons of fish a year are farmed here and sent directly to the city's numerous fish markets. Production costs are minimal, labor is local, irrigation is never a problem, refrigeration isn't required, and transport costs are negligible. In essence, the Wetlands turn negatives into positives and are a prime example of urban agriculture. But this isn't just cheap food for those who can't afford anything else. These *bheris* produce the fish that Calcutta loves, namely the carp family: *rui*, *katla*, *mirgil*, and silver carp, as well as *tilapia*; fish where nothing is wasted, where even the head ends up in a dish of dal, one of Bengal's supreme delicacies.

As if all that weren't enough, the Wetlands are also idyllic, especially considering their proximity to one of the most polluted and overcrowded metropolises known to man. The very idea of heading off for a tranquil afternoon's stroll in a place that's also a destination for raw, untreated sewage might sound contradictory. But, once in the heart of these *bheris*, there's just the faint rustling of palm leaves or the occasional flapping of an egret's wings. The light is bathed in softness; there's shade under clumps of papaya trees and birdsong from the *paancouri* hovering above. Only the silhouette of the fishermen gathering their nets provides any hint of industry.

Getting fish to market is quick — deliberately so. As far back as 1822, a committee was set up to monitor and improve fish production in the city, and reported that "fish is universally used by all classes of the inhabitants." Thus, locations such as Gariahat, Manicktala, Sealdah, and Lake Market all specialize in fish. But the choicest specimens end up at the main, centrally located New Market, which opened on New Year's Day 1874. It was renamed Hogg Market (after Sir Stuart Hogg, a municipal chairman) in 1903, but to virtually everyone it is still New Market. The brickwork and clock tower are painted a municipal shade of rusty red and the whole thing reminds me of St. Pancras Station in miniature. Inside, the fish

section is cavernous and noisy, with armies of fishmongers going about their business under the light of hundreds of naked filaments.

The firm of B.C. Ojha has been a prime mover here for more than 80 years, and today it's the turn of B.C.'s grandson, Shivaji. Le tout Calcutta knows him. Five-star hotel food and beverage managers, the most exclusive wedding caterers and the smartest hostesses all come calling. What singles out the company is its ability to supply the best-quality large estuary fish, in particular the imperious *bhetki*. Unlike the bonier sweetwater fish, the British fell upon it (calling it *bekti*) because, like certain North Atlantic white fish, once you remove the central backbone it has few others.

Shivaji's grandfather learned to filet, and thus his trade grew rapidly. "And slowly, slowly, Indian and Bengali people adopted the same system of *bhetki* without bones for baking, grilling and frying." As he explains, he slaps down a whole range of fish —Indian haddock, reef cod, Bombay *bhetki* and silver snapper — all easy to filet and perfect for the city's restaurants, tandoor ovens, and the incalculable number of portions of fish that Calcutta gobbles up on a daily basis. Much of the B.C. Ojha supply comes from the wholesale market at Canning, a town some 30 miles south of Calcutta, near the start of the Sunderbans. As with so many other fish in the world, wild estuarine *bhetki* is becoming rarer and costlier, and farmed *bhetki* ever more commonplace.

But there is one fish that rises above all others. The British adored it and smoked it, and Muslims, Hindus, Bangals, and Ghotis alike revere it. It is the delicately flavored *ilish* or *hilsa*, a member of the shad family and a fish that is best eaten during the monsoon season (June to September). "We say it comes dancing up the river when it rains," I was told. In fact, it comes in from the sea to spawn in estuaries before moving farther inland. According to R.P. Gupta in his book *Maachh Ar Bangali*, connoisseurs used to exist who could tell from its taste which *ghat* (river pier) in Calcutta the *hilsa* came from: Babu Ghat or Bagbazar Ghat and so on. He details its silver scales and likens its still eyes to transparent blue sapphires. But it is the taste, fragile yet earthy, and the pungency of ground mustard that renders the Bengali misty-eyed at the very thought of the fish that reigns supreme.

Bhapa maach paturi
Fish with mustard steamed in banana leaf

Bengalis proudly state that they are the masters of the art of using Indian brown mustard seeds and the imported Greek black mustard seeds. This claim is eloquently demonstrated by the preparation of several recipes, including this one, *shorshe bata maach,* and *bhapa eelish.* The use of ingredients is so similar that just a masterfully deft slant of technique yields a pleasantly startling different dish.

Serves 4

1lb 5oz Indian herring filets with skin, cut into 4 pieces, or boneless, skinless cod or halibut, cut into 8 pieces

1 tsp salt, plus extra to taste

2 tsp turmeric

juice of ½ lime

4–5 medium fresh green chilis

2½ tbsp each of brown and black mustard seeds

1½ cups warm water

1 tsp red chili powder

2 tbsp fresh grated coconut (optional, *see* page 159)

3 tbsp mustard oil

1 banana leaf (or parchment paper)

1 Wash the fish pieces and rub with a mixture of 1 tsp each of salt and turmeric and all the lime juice. Roughly chop 2 of the green chilis; slice the remainder lengthwise.

2 Soak the mustard seeds in ⅝ cup of the warm water for 20 minutes, then use a mortar and pestle to blend the seeds to a fine paste with the chilis, red chili powder, and grated coconut (if using). Add the remaining warm water as required. The consistency needs to be thick for coating. Fold in the mustard oil and add salt as needed.

3 Cut the banana leaf into 6-inch squares (or the parchment paper into 8-inch squares for the cod or halibut). Place the herring filet on the leaf, coat liberally with the mustard paste, place a slice of green chili on top, and fold the leaf over to make a closed packet. Secure this with kitchen string. In the case of cod or halibut, dip the fish in the paste, add the chilis in the same way, coat well and wrap similarly.

4 Steam the fish for 10–12 minutes in a conventional steamer. Or, to create a sensation, bury the fish parcels in freshly cooked, steaming-hot basmati rice for 20 minutes. Then give it 2 minutes in a hot oven to be absolutely sure it's cooked and serve as is with the rice.

5 Another way Bengalis cook this fish is by wrapping it in about five layers of banana leaves and then cooking in a hot frying pan, turning the parcels over a couple of times and allowing the leaves to char as the fish cooks. You will need to fry it for 5–6 minutes before finishing it off in a hot oven for 3 minutes. Cooked this way, I call this delicacy simply *maach paturi.*

◣ Doi maach
Fish with yogurt

Use bigger fish cut into pieces for this dish, rather than small fish. Yogurt does not make a strong sauce, so the fish should not be too strong in flavor. Bengalis would use carp or *bhetki*, but you can use a white fish with flaky flesh such as cod or haddock.

Serves 4

1lb 12oz skinless white fish filet (cod, haddock) or carp steaks, scaled

½ tsp salt, plus extra to taste

3 tsp turmeric

2½ cups plain yogurt

1 tbsp chickpea flour

½ tsp red chili powder

½ tsp ground cumin

2 tsp sugar

mustard oil

1 large dried bay leaf

1 small onion, peeled and finely chopped

2 medium fresh green chilis, cut lengthwise in half (optional)

1 Wash the fish, and rub it with ½ tsp salt and 1 tsp of turmeric. Set the fish aside.

2 Using a whisk, mix the yogurt with the chickpea flour, remaining turmeric, red chili powder, cumin, and sugar. Taste to see whether the sugar-salt balance needs adjusting and add more sugar or salt as needed.

3 In a wide pan, fry the pieces of fish in mustard oil on both sides for a few minutes. Remove and then set aside.

4 Strain the oil through a fine sieve, return to the same pan and reheat. Add the bay leaf and onion, and fry until light brown. Add the spiced yogurt and simmer on a low heat for about 15 minutes.

5 Arrange the fish pieces in the sauce, coat them, and simmer for a few minutes more. If using, add the fresh chilis to the sauce at this point for extra heat and aroma. (East Bengalis would prefer to add the chilis; West Bengalis are happy just with a sweet-and-sour taste.) Serve with boiled rice.

Morola maach bhaja
Spiced whitebait

In Bengal, the fish we can get are so small that you can hear them crunch as you eat them. Here whitebait are a bit larger, so after the initial crunch you have a soft center. Serve this dish on its own, as a first course or as an accompaniment to rice and dal.

Serves 4

14oz whitebait

coarse-grained salt

juice of 1 lime

1 tsp turmeric

2 tsp red chili powder

1 tsp ground cumin

½-inch piece fresh ginger, peeled and roughly chopped

3 garlic cloves, peeled and roughly chopped

1⅓ cup plus 1 tbsp all-purpose flour

1⅓ cup plus 1 tbsp chickpea flour

1 tbsp rice flour

fine-grained salt

4 tbsp vegetable oil

1 Put the whitebait in a dish, and rub with a little coarse-grained salt; this removes any scales and cleans them. Wash and drain well, then rub with the lime juice and ground spices.

2 Grind the ginger and garlic to a paste in a mortar. Mix the 3 flours with this paste and add fine-grained salt to taste. Toss the fish in this coating.

3 Heat the vegetable oil in a *karai* or heavy wok and fry the fish in batches over a medium heat until crisp. This should take about 8–10 minutes each time. Drain well and serve hot.

Bhapa eelish
Steamed Indian herring with mustard

The unique flavor of the Indian herring is highlighted in this dish. Bengalis adore fried fish, but the combination of mustard and *hilsa* is appreciated best when steamed as here.

1 Cut the herring into 4 steaks, or the halibut into 8 pieces. Rub with 1 tsp each of the salt and turmeric and then set aside.

2 Wash and soak the mustard seeds in the warm water for 20 minutes, then put the seeds with some water in the blender with 2 of the green chilis, roughly chopped, the remaining turmeric and salt as needed. Blend to a fine paste, adding a little extra water if necessary.

3 Dip the fish pieces into the paste to coat on all sides. Arrange the pieces in a shallow dish that will fit into the top part of your steamer. Drizzle the mustard oil on top, and add the remaining chilis, cut lengthwise in half. Cover the steamer very tightly, and steam the fish for 15 minutes, or until cooked. Serve with boiled rice.

Serves 4

1lb 12oz Indian herring with skin or skinless halibut filet

1 tsp salt, plus extra to taste

2 tsp turmeric

4 tbsp brown mustard seeds

about 1 cup warm water

6 medium fresh green chilis

2 tbsp mustard oil

A Wetlands fisherman preparing to take his
catch to market.

⚔ *Bhaja golda chingri*
Spiced pan-fried shrimp

Freshwater shrimp are widely available just before the monsoon in Bengal. They are about 8–10 inches long, and a treat for the Bengalis. The Bengali housewife would fry the shrimp heads separately for the more adventurous members of the family; you eat the shell and everything!

Serves 4

8 colossal shrimp, heads and shells removed

½ tsp salt, plus extra as needed

3 tsp turmeric

1 small red onion, peeled and roughly chopped

2-inch piece fresh ginger, peeled and chopped

2 tsp red chili powder

2 tsp ground cumin

1 tsp garam masala (*see* page 21)

½ tsp sugar

juice of 1 lemon

all-purpose flour

vegetable oil

1 Wash and devein the shrimp and slit them open (or butterfly) along the back curve (do not split completely). Beat the shrimp gently open with the blunt edge of a knife; this prevents them from curling up during frying. Rub with ½ tsp salt and 1 tsp turmeric and then set aside.

2 Grind the red onion and ginger to a fine paste in the blender and add the red chili powder, ground cumin, the remaining turmeric, the garam masala, sugar, and a pinch of salt with the lemon juice. Rub the shrimp with this paste, then sprinkle with all-purpose flour.

3 Heat some vegetable oil in a shallow pan and pan-fry the shrimp on both sides until golden, about 5–6 minutes. Drain well, and serve with a wedge of lemon and perhaps some *khashundi* (*see* page 190).

Chingri maacher malai curry
Shrimp and coconut curry

When you get a tender coconut in the market, the next thing to look for is some good fresh shrimp, for this combination is classic. The sweetness of the coconut perfectly matches the sweetness of the shrimp, and the hint of fresh green chilis adds a unique dimension.

Serves 4

1 fresh coconut

2lb 4oz medium shrimp, shelled and deveined

1 tsp salt, plus extra to taste

3 tsp turmeric

⅛ cup mustard oil

2 medium onions, peeled and roughly chopped

1-inch piece fresh ginger, peeled and chopped

5 garlic cloves, peeled and chopped

3 medium fresh green chilis

½ tsp red chili powder

2 tsp brown mustard seeds, soaked in warm water to cover

½ tsp sugar

1 Crack open the coconut and grate the flesh. Make thick and thin coconut milk as described on page 136. Keep the residue.

2 Wash the shrimp, and rub with 1 tsp each of the salt and turmeric. Set aside.

3 Heat the mustard oil in a shallow pan, and fry the shrimp rapidly to sear on all sides. Remove, then strain the oil through a fine sieve back into the pan.

4 Put the onion, ginger, garlic, green chilis, red chili powder, and coconut residue into a blender, and add the mustard seeds, not adding too much of their liquid. Blend to a very fine paste.

5 Reheat the oil and add the paste. Fry very well, for about 15 minutes, stirring all the time.

6 Add the thin coconut milk first, with the sugar. Bring to a simmer, and add the shrimp. Cook gently for another 3–4 minutes, then add the thick coconut milk. Check the salt, adding a little more if necessary, and simmer for a couple more minutes. Serve with boiled rice.

⚑ Lau chingri
Small shrimp with bottle gourd

Bottle gourd is a green, round, bottle-shaped, marrow-like vegetable. In India it is also known as *lau, lauki,* or *dudhi.* The peelings make a great vegetarian stir-fry with dried red chilis, which my grandma insisted on so that nothing was wasted. The soft core with the seeds was transformed into fritters with ground yellow chickpeas. The fleshy part reigned supreme, cooked with plump shrimp.

Serves 4

28 small shrimp (about 9oz)

1 tsp salt, plus extra to taste

1 tbsp turmeric

1lb 5oz bottle gourd

2 tbsp mustard oil

½ tsp cumin seeds

2–3 dried bay leaves

2 tsp ground cumin

2–3 tsp red chili powder

3 medium fresh green chilis, cut lengthwise

½ cup hot water

2 tsp all-purpose flour or finely ground uncooked rice

½ tsp sugar

3–4 sprigs fresh cilantro, chopped

1 Wash the shrimp and rub with 1 tsp each of salt and turmeric.

2 Peel the gourd, cut it in half lengthwise and remove the soft core. Cut the firm part into fine pieces (like thickly grated carrots).

3 Heat the mustard oil in a *karai* or heavy wok to very hot, add the shrimp and stir-fry rapidly for a minute. Remove from the *karai.* Reheat the remaining oil, add the cumin seeds and brown for 30 seconds. Add the bay leaves, the cut gourd, the remaining turmeric, the cumin, the red chili powder, and the green chilis. Stir well and cook for 20–25 minutes, adding hot water a little at a time to allow the gourd to become very soft.

4 Put in the stir-fried shrimp, the all-purpose flour, sugar, and some salt as needed, mix well and continue to cook for 5–7 minutes to allow the flour to cook and to give the dish a full body and glistening appearance.

5 Serve topped with fresh cilantro and accompanied by steaming-hot rice or *luchis* (*see* page 66).

cutting techniques are core characteristics of Bengali cuisine, fundamental to the specific flavor of a dish.

A satisfactory explanation of these methods is elusive. Bengalis love to throw up smokescreens and construct a mystique, whether it's in the inspiration behind their poetry, the way the dew settles on far-flung stretches of land in ancestral tracts of east Bengal, or the methodology and romance attached to a winter dish such as *matar dal* (yellow split peas), with its additions of potatoes, *patol*, pumpkin, and *mooli*. Some people blind you with science, detailing the way a vegetable is cut, the surface area exposed, and the amount of oxidation allowed, linked to the cooking time. The gist is that finely cut ingredients need to be cooked quickly and immediately and the required spices shouldn't need long in which to blend. When cut larger, ingredients need more cooking time and spices that can mellow over a longer period.

Other characteristics crop up regularly. Many dishes involve the twin additions of sugar and salt. Why? "I put in sugar purely to bring out the taste of the salt," Rakhi DasGupta tells me. Then, there's a determination to waste nothing. Fish heads cooked with dal or rice (*see* page 31) are seen as a delicacy and fish bones are picked, chewed, and sucked until virtually nothing remains. Likewise, there are dishes such as *khosha chorchori* that turn bits of stalk, outer leaves, and vegetable peelings into refined statements that are greater than the sum of their parts.

Another trait is a fondness for bitter tastes, and this is shared less frequently by non-Bengalis. In her book *Life and Food in Bengal*, Chitrita Banerji describes being directed by her mother to swallow bitter gourds and a *shukto* made with a mixture of vegetables including the "excruciatingly bitter leaves of the *patol*." After a childhood of being force-fed, she now concedes that "nothing tastes sweeter." Much of this thinking stems from the unshakeable belief — now lost in many areas of the West — in food as medicine, linked back to the principles of the Ayurveda. Indians in general refer frequently to the properties of foods and dishes as having of either a "heating" or a "cooling" nature. Once, in high summer, I was berated by a friend of mine: "Why are you eating eggs for breakfast? They heat the body far too much. You need cooling preparations."

Thus, foods are known for their direct effect on the body. According to Rakhi DasGupta, "We believe that bitter things take care of everything — diabetes, tummy troubles, the lot. We truly are a nation of hypochrondriacs and get paranoid about illness, so we've developed a taste for bitter items, especially throughout the summer months."

Finally, there's a branch of vegetable cooking called "widow's food." Rakhi Sarcar — a director of Calcutta's CIMA (Centre for International Modern Art) Gallery in Sunny Park, Ballygunge — explains that, historically, Bengal was a polygamous society with many young girls marrying much older men. As the men died, these girls often became widows very early on, and as such their lot was not a happy one. They dressed only in white saris and they were not allowed access to the main kitchen of a house. The feeling was, "you've killed off your husband, therefore you mustn't tamper with what we eat." They were restricted in what they could eat: no meat, fish, onion, garlic, nor certain sorts of lentils — in fact, anything that was considered to possess an aphrodisiac quality and promote physical thoughts or stirrings. Thus, widows developed a cuisine of their own: one that required great ingenuity and resulted in great nuances, due to the sheer weight of the restrictions placed on them by society until 100 or so years ago. In fact, in his novel *Chokher Bali*, Rabindranath Tagore's character Binodini, a young widow, is praised for "her cooking, her ways, her speech." And as far as Rakhi Sarcar is concerned, it was women like that who took Bengali cooking to such a level of finesse and who have given it one of its most enduring strands.

:: Begun shorshe
Eggplant with yogurt and mustard

Butter-soft baby eggplants are fried and doused with fresh ground mustard and yogurt sauce, and tempered with panch phoran. Baby eggplants are seasonal — if you cannot get any just use larger ones cut into long slices.

1 Trim the stalks and cut the eggplants lengthwise into quarters without cutting through at the stalk. Rub about ½ tsp of salt and 2 tsp of turmeric into the insides of the eggplants, then fry them in medium-hot vegetable oil until soft and almost cooked. This should take about 4 minutes and they should turn shiny bright purple. Set aside on absorbent paper towels.

2 Soak the mustard seeds in 2 tbsp warm water for 10 minutes, then grind to a smooth paste in a blender. Remove and reserve. Put the remaining turmeric, the red chili powder, garlic, and ginger with 1 tbsp water in the blender and whiz to form a paste. Using a whisk, blend the yogurt with the chickpea flour, sugar, and ½ tsp salt.

3 For the panch phoran, select good-quality, dust-free spices. Combine well and store in an airtight jar.

4 Reheat 2 tbsp of the oil to hot in a saucepan and add the chilis and the panch phoran. When the spices crackle, add the ginger-garlic paste and stir-fry for 2 minutes. Reduce the heat slightly and add the yogurt mix. Bring to a simmer, gently working with a whisk (if it boils the yogurt tends to split), and check the sugar-salt balance, adjusting as needed. Mix in the mustard paste, then carefully lay the eggplants in the sauce.

5 Sprinkle with fresh cilantro, cover the pan, and simmer for 2 minutes. Serve with boiled rice.

Serves 4

8 baby eggplants (those with few or no seeds)

1 tsp salt, divided

3 tsp turmeric

4 tbsp vegetable oil

1½ tbsp black mustard seeds

2 tsp red chili powder (or to taste)

4 garlic cloves, peeled

½-inch piece fresh ginger, peeled

1 cup plain yogurt

1 tbsp chickpea flour

2 tsp sugar

4 medium fresh green chilis, cut lengthwise in half

1 tsp panch phoran (*see* below)

2–3 sprigs fresh cilantro, chopped

Panch phoran

1 tbsp plus 1 tsp cumin seeds

1 tbsp fennel seeds

2 tsp nigella seeds

2 tsp brown mustard seeds

½ tsp fenugreek seeds

Begun bhaja
Fried eggplant

At certain points during the phase of the moon, Bengalis are vegetarian. A lot of emphasis is put on vegetarian dishes, and interesting combinations are used to make wholesome vegetarian meals. Fish appears occasionally, while meat would be restricted to Sunday or special occasions. This dish is perfect for breakfast with *luchis* or served at the start of a meal with other fried vegetables.

Serves 4

1 tsp turmeric

½ tsp salt

2 medium eggplants, cut into ¼-inch-thick rounds

1 tbsp all-purpose flour

mustard oil

1 Rub the turmeric and salt into the eggplant rounds, and sprinkle a little water over to moisten them. Dust with the all-purpose flour.

2 Heat the mustard oil in a shallow frying pan until smoking. Allow to cool slightly, then add the eggplant rounds in batches, turning them once they are golden brown on one side, and frying until golden brown on the other. The finished eggplant should have a soft center and a crisp skin.

3 This must be eaten straight from the pan, and is best with *luchis* (*see page 66*).

tip: There are two ways in which to judge whether your eggplant is suitable for this dish. The eggplant should not be too firm when pressed; and when tapped with your fingernails, there should not be a hollow sound.

Aloo posto
Potatoes with poppy seeds

In some homes turmeric is used purely for visual reasons, so some recipes include it with the poppy seeds, or it can be used while frying the potatoes, as here. When ridge cucumbers are in season in winter, Bengalis use these rather than potatoes. They are partly scraped of their ridges, then cut into 1-inch cubes, added to the dish just after the onions have browned, and stir-fried for less than a minute.

Serves 4

2 tbsp poppy seeds

salt

½-inch piece fresh ginger, peeled and chopped

3–4 medium fresh green chilis, roughly chopped

3 tbsp vegetable oil

3 medium potatoes, peeled and cut into lengthwise wedges, about ½ inch thick

1 tsp turmeric (optional)

2 medium whole dried red chilis, torn into small pieces

a pinch of sugar

1 medium onion, peeled, halved, and sliced

1 Soak the poppy seeds in warm water, just to cover, for at least an hour. Blend them with a pinch of salt to as fine a paste as possible. Separately grind the ginger and chilis to a rough paste.

2 Heat the vegetable oil in a *karai* or heavy wok over low heat. Rub the potato wedges with turmeric (if using); this gives the dish a brighter color. Pan-fry the wedges, in two batches if required, until golden and crisp — about 8–10 minutes. They don't need to be completely cooked at this stage.

3 Strain the oil and put 1 tbsp back into the pan. Fry the chilis, sugar, and onion until light brown. Add the ginger-chili paste and fry for a minute, then add the poppy seed paste. Cook, stirring continuously, for 2–3 minutes, then add about 4 tbsp water. Add the potatoes and cook for another 8–10 minutes, adding another 2 tbsp water if required. Check for seasoning, and add more salt as needed.

4 The finished dish should have a fairly thick consistency. It is best served with boiled rice and a wedge of lime for each person.

tip: Poppy seeds are notoriously difficult to grind to a paste. This is why they should be soaked in water, which softens them. A little coarse-grained salt added to them when grinding helps break them up.

Kancha aamer jhol
Green mango curry

This is a summer cooler, made when the mangoes are unripe and green on the trees before the rains start. The strain of mangoes used for this are not best enjoyed as ripe fruit. The *jhol* is usually eaten toward the end of the meal, without rice or other accompaniments, as a palate freshener. But if it is a Sunday meal — that is, slightly more elaborate — fried poppadums would be served with it.

Serves 4

3 medium green mangoes

1-inch piece fresh ginger, peeled

1 medium fresh green chili, roughly chopped

1 tbsp mustard oil

1 tsp panch phoran (*see* page 54)

2 dried red chilis, broken into small pieces (hot) or left whole (less hot)

1 tsp turmeric

1 tbsp ground coriander

½ tsp ground cumin

1 tbsp sugar

about 2¼ cups water

salt, to taste

1 Peel the mangoes and cut them into ½-inch wedges lengthwise. If the stone is hard, cut around it but don't discard it; if the stone is soft, cut through it and discard the inner seed (the soft casing is edible). Grind the ginger and fresh chili to a paste in a mortar and pestle.

2 Heat the mustard oil to hot in a heavy wok or *karai*. Add the panch phoran and dried chilis and allow to crackle. Add the ginger-chili paste, the turmeric, coriander, and cumin. Fry rapidly for a minute, then add about 1 tbsp water, just to prevent sticking. Add the sugar, mango pieces, and mango stones, and fry for 3–4 minutes.

3 Add the remaining water. Bring this to a boil, then simmer until the mango is soft. The timing will vary depending on the type of mango, but it should take 10–12 minutes, by which time the mangoes will be breaking up.

4 Taste and adjust the sweet-salt balance. Serve at room temperature. The stones in the relish are the fun part of it, which children like to linger over and suck; they are not eaten.

Kumro chenchki
Stir-fried pumpkin and dried chilis

This autumnal dish is made with what Bengalis call red pumpkin, which is in fact the same as the Halloween pumpkin. It should be young on the vine, with the skin still soft and edible. This is usually eaten to whet the appetite at the beginning of a meal.

Serves 4

1 tbsp mustard oil

3 medium dried red chilis, broken into small pieces

½ tsp panch phoran (*see* page 54)

½-inch piece fresh ginger, peeled and ground to a paste

about 4 cups pumpkin, cleaned of seeds and fibers, skin on, cut into ½-inch pieces

½ tsp sugar

1 tsp turmeric

½ tsp red chili powder

1 tbsp ground coriander

½ tsp ground cumin

1 cup water

salt

1 Heat the mustard oil in a *karai* or heavy wok until smoking. Let it cool slightly, then add the chilis and panch phoran and allow to crackle. Add the ginger paste, and fry for a minute, then add the pumpkin, sugar, and ground spices. Stir-fry for 2–3 minutes.

2 Add the water, and cook for another 5–6 minutes, until the pumpkin is soft but not breaking up. Add salt to taste, and then check the sweet-salt balance. Serve with boiled rice or *luchis* (*see* page 66).

⬚⬚ Cholar dal
Yellow split peas with coconut and golden raisins

Serves 4

2 cups yellow split peas, well rinsed, soaked for 3 hours, and drained

salt

1 tsp turmeric

½ tsp red chili powder

2 tsp sugar

¼ fresh coconut (*see* page 159)

2 tbsp vegetable oil

4 round dried red chilis (available in Asian shops as *boor mirch*)

2 tsp panch phoran (*see* page 54)

2 dried bay leaves

2 tbsp golden raisins

3–4 sprigs fresh cilantro, chopped

This is a festive Bengali dish favored for wedding banquets and as an offering during religious ceremonies. Coconut, golden raisins, sugar, and salt combine to give a wonderful balance, which my mother got perfect every time. This dal is best enjoyed with *luchis*.

1 Put the drained yellow split peas in a large, deep saucepan and add enough boiling water to just cover the split peas. Bring to a boil, then reduce to a simmer. Skim off and discard the froth. Add salt to taste, the turmeric, red chili powder, and sugar. Simmer the split peas until they are still defined but soft, about 20 minutes, adding more hot water if required. Now lightly mash the split peas to break them up partly and give it some body. Set this aside.

2 Meanwhile, carefully pry loose the white flesh of the coconut with a strong knife, and chop it into small pieces.

3 Heat the vegetable oil in a small frying pan. When it is almost smoking hot, add the red chilis and panch phoran. It should crackle in 10 seconds. Now throw in the bay leaves, coconut pieces, and golden raisins. Swirl the oil around until the coconut turns golden and the golden raisins puff up.

4 Pour this sizzling mix over the split peas, and cover it immediately with a tight-fitting lid. While the flavors soak in, put the saucepan back on the heat and bring to a simmer. Mix in the oil and flavorings, and adjust the seasoning.

5 Sprinkle the fresh cilantro on top and serve with hot *luchis* (*see* page 66).

Misti polao
Festive rice

This is a sweetened, aromatic rice dish, reserved for an indulgent Sunday lunch or a family celebration. It is eaten as a savory part of the main meal. The sweetness (from caramelized sugar) complements the more robust spicing of the meat and vegetable dishes. In Bengal, basmati rice would not normally be used for this; a short-grain, local rice would be preferred.

Serves 4

3⅔ cups basmati rice, washed

a handful of shelled cashew nuts

2 tbsp raisins

3 tbsp ghee

2-inch cinnamon stick, broken

3–4 cloves

3–4 green cardamoms

1 small piece mace

2 tsp sugar

1 small cauliflower, broken into small florets

salt

Crisp fried onions

salt

2 medium onions, peeled, halved, and sliced

vegetable oil

1 Preheat the oven to 350°F. Cover the rice, nuts, and raisins separately with warm water to soak.

2 Meanwhile, for the crisp fried onions, sprinkle ½ tsp of salt on the sliced onions, and leave for 5 minutes. Squeeze out any excess liquid. Loosen the onion slices and spread them on a piece of absorbent paper towel. Heat the vegetable oil in a *karai* or heavy wok, and deep-fry the sliced onion in batches until light golden in color. Remove and drain, spreading out on more paper towels; the onion will continue coloring to a rich golden brown, and the pieces will be crisp. Set aside for the garnish. (The onion can be stored in airtight containers for a few months.)

3 Heat the ghee in a casserole dish with a tight-fitting lid on the stovetop over medium heat. Add the spices and fry for less than a minute (just enough time to release their aromas). Add the sugar and lightly caramelize, then add the cauliflower florets and the soaked and drained nuts and raisins. When the nuts have browned slightly, add the rice and fry for a minute or so. Add enough water to cover the rice and cauliflower by about 1 inch, and some salt to taste.

4 Simmer, stirring occasionally, until the water is almost absorbed. Cover and put in the oven for 20 minutes.

5 Remove from the oven, let stand for 2 minutes, then loosen the rice with a flat spoon to aerate it before it gets lumpy.

6 Serve the rice topped with the crisp fried onions.

▪▪ Khichuri
Rice, lentils, and vegetables

A *khichuri* (the word means a mishmash) is a convenience meal for when time is short or markets are difficult to get to, especially during the monsoon. It's a wholesome all-in-one dish, because nothing is drained away and all the nutrients are retained. The combinations used in *khichuris* are practically limitless, and the principle is a mix of carbohydrates, proteins, and fiber.

Serves 4

2¼ cups broken basmati rice, washed and soaked for 30 minutes and drained

½ cup red lentils, washed and soaked

½ cup yellow lentils, washed and soaked

2 tsp turmeric

2 medium potatoes, peeled and quartered

1 cup hot water

1 small cauliflower, broken into small florets

1 cup French beans, strings removed, cut into 1-inch pieces

3 medium tomatoes

salt

a pinch of sugar

Phoran

2 tbsp vegetable oil

1 tsp cumin seeds

½-inch piece fresh ginger, peeled and finely chopped

1 medium fresh green chili, cut lengthwise

1 Put the soaked and drained rice and lentils into a deep saucepan with the turmeric and pour in enough water to cover the ingredients by 1½ inches. Bring to a boil and simmer for about 10 minutes, until the rice and lentils start softening.

2 Add the potatoes, and cook for another 10 minutes, until the rice is almost soft. Add the hot water along with the cauliflower, beans, and tomatoes, some salt, and the sugar. Stir occasionally and allow the rice and lentils to start breaking up, about another 10 minutes, when the potatoes will be fully cooked. Add 1 tbsp water occasionally if needed. The consistency should be similar to a loose porridge.

3 Heat the 2 tbsp vegetable oil for the phoran in a small pan over medium heat. Add the cumin, ginger, and chili, and fry until the cumin seeds crackle. Pour this oil over the rice and lentils and mix it in.

4 Serve the dish steaming hot with fried poppadums or fried fish (*see* page 38).

Ghee bhaat
Boiled rice flavored with ghee

Bengalis are fond of milk and its products. Ghee is the most aromatic milk product, and a simple dish like boiled rice is transformed to a delicacy by the addition of it. The rice is also often used as a vehicle for cooking vegetables such as potatoes and beans, which are served separately, spiced with a little fresh chili and mustard and eaten with this dish.

Serves 4

salt

3⅔ cups long-grain rice, washed and soaked for about 20 minutes

2 tbsp ghee

1 Boil a large pan of water, add salt to taste, and the drained softened rice. Pour off any excess water, leaving about 1 inch above the rice. (Any vegetables would be added at this point, *see* above.) Bring to a boil, then simmer until the water has almost been absorbed, about 6–8 minutes.

2 Add the ghee, and gently mix it in. (Remove the vegetables at this stage.) Now cover the pan and leave on a very slow heat for about 3–4 minutes, until all the excess moisture has evaporated.

3 Loosen the rice using a flat spoon, and serve with the lightly spiced vegetables, if using, or any mild curries.

Palong shager ghonto
Spinach with mixed vegetables

This is a winter dish, and is one way of getting your family to eat spinach (it's not a dish for entertaining). To entice the younger members of the family, vegetables such as pumpkins, sweet potatoes, and eggplants are added to the spinach. One thing we might add here is sun-dried lentil dumplings, *bori* or *vadi*, which bring about a balance of nutrients. (You can buy these ready-made in Asian shops.)

Serves 4

about 4 cups fresh spinach

2 medium sweet potatoes

1 medium potato

1 small pumpkin

1 small eggplant

2 tsp cumin seeds

1 tbsp coriander seeds

2 whole red dried chilis, seeded

1-inch piece fresh ginger, peeled and chopped

2 tbsp vegetable oil

1 tsp turmeric

½ tsp sugar

salt

1 Wash the spinach. Peel the potatoes and pumpkin and cut them into ½-inch cubes. Cut the eggplant into ½-inch cubes as well.

2 Put 1 tsp of cumin seeds and all the coriander seeds and red chilis in a spice mill and grind to a fine powder. Mix the powder into the chopped ginger and grind to make a paste.

3 Heat the vegetable oil in a *karai* or heavy wok over medium heat, add the remaining cumin seeds, and fry until they crackle, brown and crisp. Add the spice-ginger paste and the turmeric, fry for a couple of minutes, then add the spinach, vegetable cubes, and sugar. Fry for 2–3 minutes.

4 Add enough water just to cover the vegetables, and cook at a simmer until all the vegetables are soft and starting to break up, about 8–10 minutes. The consistency should be quite thick. Add salt to taste, and check the sugar-salt balance.

5 Serve with boiled rice. Fresh green chilis can be added if you like a bit of heat.

Luchi
Deep-fried bread

Luchi is referred to as *poori* in other parts of India. Well-made *luchis* go down so rapidly that often you are embarrassed to count how many you have eaten. As a child I loved to poke a hole in a hot *luchi* and watch the smoke swirl out as it cooled. Bengalis enjoy *luchis* with *cholar dal* (yellow split peas with coconut and golden raisins; *see* page 60).

Makes 12

2 cups all-purpose flour

salt

2 tsp vegetable oil

about ¼ cup tepid water

vegetable oil

1 To make the dough, sift the all-purpose flour into a mixing bowl and add a little salt to taste. Rub in the 2 tsp vegetable oil and add the water gradually and cautiously. Knead to a malleable but firm dough. Cover with a moist cloth and let rest for 15 minutes.

2 Divide the dough into 12 equal-size balls. Heat the oil in a *karai* or heavy wok to smoking hot, then slightly reduce the heat to maintain optimum temperature. Roll out the balls of dough very thinly on a lightly floured or oiled surface. Fry one *luchi* at a time quickly, flipping over in about 30 seconds. Carefully splash hot oil onto the bread and watch it balloon. Remove each *luchi* from the oil and drain. Fry them all and enjoy them hot. (*Luchis* cannot be reheated back to their original fluffiness or crispness.)

Tomato aar kacha aamer chutney
Ripe tomato and green mango chutney

Bengalis relish this chutney with or without fried poppadoms after main courses, and before seriously tucking into the desserts. No matter how expertly each dish is executed by the cook, no Bengali will praise the meal if the chutney is missing. So it's certainly worth learning this dish.

Serves 6–8

9 small ripe red tomatoes, halved

5 unripe green mangoes, peeled, stoned, and diced

½ cup raisins

½-inch piece fresh ginger, peeled and finely chopped

4 tsp grated jaggery

1½ tbsp sugar

½ tsp red chili powder

½ tsp turmeric

salt

2 tbsp mustard oil

2 tsp panch phoran (*see* page 54)

2 whole dried red chilis, broken in half and seeded

1 Put ½ cup water into a large saucepan, and add the tomatoes, mangoes, raisins, ginger, jaggery, sugar, red chili powder, and turmeric. Bring to a boil, then simmer for 30 minutes, stirring frequently and adding a little water if required, until the tomatoes are fully cooked and soft. Mix in salt to taste. The consistency should be thick, and the tomatoes should have broken up and blended with the other ingredients. Remove from heat.

2 Heat the mustard oil to smoking hot in a small pan, cool a little, then throw in the panch phoran and chilis. When they crackle, pour the oil and spice mix over the chutney and stir in thoroughly.

3 This chutney is best enjoyed at room temperature with some fried poppadums.

Anarosher chutney
Ripe pineapple chutney

Makes about 1½ cups

2 medium ripe pineapples

⅓ cup plus 1 tbsp grated jaggery

⅓ cup plus 1 tbsp sugar

2 tbsp raisins

½ tsp red chili powder

½-inch piece fresh ginger, peeled and chopped

salt

about 2 cups water

2 tbsp vegetable oil

2 medium whole dried red chilis, seeded and cut into small pieces

2 tsp panch phoran (*see* page 54)

This chutney is made when pineapples are toward the end of their season and in abundance. Overripe pineapples are best, and the chutney is served toward the end of the meal, before the desserts, sometimes with fried poppadums or as a relish. It keeps well, and can be stored in the fridge for a few weeks. Serve at room temperature or chilled.

1 Peel the pineapples, remove the eyes, and cut the flesh into ½-inch cubes. Put into a deep saucepan with the jaggery, sugar, raisins, red chili powder, ginger, and salt to taste. Cook gently to melt the sugar and jaggery. Once they melt and caramelize and are just starting to turn color, add the water and simmer for 15–20 minutes. The pineapple pieces should start to disintegrate. Keep cooking, stirring with a wooden spoon, until the pineapple has broken down, which could take another 40 minutes. The consistency should become like a medium-thick jam. Once this stage is reached, check the sugar-salt balance and adjust as needed.

2 Heat the vegetable oil in a small frying pan until smoking hot. Cool a little, then add the chilis and panch phoran, and cook until they crackle. Pour immediately over the chutney. Mix in well.

THE RAJ

Get past the security checkpoint at the entrance to the Tollygunge Club and you're forced to do a quick left turn and follow alongside a long, wide concrete ramp as it slowly emerges out of the ground. This is the roof of the tunnel of the most southerly point of India's first underground metropolitan railway line. You stay parallel with it for a hundred yards or so before the system pushes ahead to the station platforms and the driveway winds off in a different direction, past ugly sponsorship hoardings and banks of canna lilies to the motley cluster of buildings known simply as "Tolly." Indeed, that bastion of le tout Calcutta at the height of the Raj was subsequently forced to shave off part of its demesne, and change its entrance and approach to make way for the clanking infrastructure of modern independent India.

Considering how long aspiring members wait, year-in, year-out, to get vetted by the membership committee, Tolly, architecturally speaking, is a pretty ramshackle affair. There's functional Tolly Towers, the icy chintz of the Belvedere Room, the funny little cake shop, and the corporate swank of the larger golf shop. Only the indoor swimming pool and the old main clubhouse building, one with its lofty proportions and the other with its portico entrance, summon up the empire spirit of the Raj.

The main clubhouse — originally built for an indigo planter — became the Tollygunge Club in 1895 and, until a few years ago, had a first-floor drawing room that was one of the most elegant and understated on the subcontinent. Also, until recently, two pictures used to face each other at the entrance: Annigoni's portrait of Queen Elizabeth II on one side and the president of India on the other. Now all that's been swept away as the building has slipped into the grim hands of an interior designer unused to such things. What's left is the plaque listing the club's presidents from W.D. Cruickshank in 1895 to the present day. Although independent India dates from 1947, change at oh-so-patrician Tolly came late and the first Indian president of the club, Brigadier R.B. Chopra, only assumed control in 1969.

Another remnant of the past at Tolly is the food — never paid for straight away, but signed off by way of a billet-doux. The late Bob Wright, for many years the club's managing member, once described to me the tea that would be set out on the lawn, its tablecloth groaning with drop scones, jams, and chocolate cake, and urns full of Margaret Hope Estate Darjeeling tea. At the Shamiana (or main club bar or 19th green), the thick, laminated menu lists standard British breakfast items, from cornflakes to bacon, eggs, and sausage to toast (although Tolly bearers always seem to refer to the latter as "*toastbutterjam*"). And then there are curiously named foods called "Jaffles": toasted chicken, cheese, and ham sandwiches only available on weekends and public holidays (and, according to the menu, only between 2 P.M. and 7 P.M.).

The real timewarp is the Belvedere Room, with its menu of cream of almond soup, *beckti duxelles,* and mango soufflé. Come Christmas, Bengali members flock in to gorge themselves on roast turkey and plum pudding. And as they sit at their table, they can gaze out upon the fairway of the 18th hole, with its tropical recreation of Godalming Golf Club, safe in the knowledge that they've bought into a strata of life, "a rigid code of manners," according to the club's publication, *A Tollygunge Club Perspective.* Safe, too, in the knowledge that thousands more are still on the outside, forced to wait that bit longer to taste the watery indifference of the almond soup.

Make no mistake: Calcuttans are a clubbable lot and that club culture is a direct manifestation of British rule. Regardless of whether they were social or sporting or both, clubs mushroomed in the 18th and 19th centuries. One Englishman wrote of them affording "some consolation for the pains of exile and loneliness." The Racing Club advertised races from 1780 onward, and then, in 1803, merged with the Jockey Club to form the new Bengal Jockey Club. In 1827, the Bengal Club was established and, under its first president Lt. Col. The Hon. J. Finch, drew up a list limited to 500 members drawn only from "civil servants of five years' service; Officers of His Majesty's Military Service; the bench, bar and clergy, on their arrival in the country."

Long-gone are the more outré clubs such as the Golden Slipper Club and the 300 Club that was kept open until dawn by Boris Lisanovitch, a White Russian. But you can still take your pick from the Calcutta Swimming Club, the Calcutta Cricket &

Football Club ("CC & FC"), the Royal Calcutta Golf Club, the Saturday Club, the Calcutta Rowing Club, and the Dalhousie Institute, as well as new additions such as the Circle Club out toward the airport (created, presumably, for those people bored with waiting on lists elsewhere).

Although invented to cushion the harshness of life in the tropics, clubs pretty much ended up replicating similar institutions back home, and a definite system of hierarchy imposed itself on who could join which club. Just below the apex, even today, nudges the Calcutta Club where, as Geoffrey Moorhouse wrote, "They were always more civil to the natives of the country, and the main staircase is hung with photographs of club presidents whose faces have from the start carefully been alternately white and brown." But still ruling supreme, even though the colonial elite has given way to captains of industry, is the Bengal Club with its symbol of the Nagraj: the king cobra.

Perhaps here more than anywhere else in the city, you can see first-hand the culinary riches of a style of cooking that of late has become much maligned. Afroze Randerian, one of the first lady members and on the food committee since 1992, invited me up to the hushed Reynolds Room, where the roar of traffic was no more than a faint hush. She explained that it was the British memsahibs who originally taught the cooks, with recipes that had been filtered through several sets of circumstances. What recipes had they brought with them? How well did they train their armies of cooks? Were their cooks Mogs from the Chittagong Hill Tracts, as they had a reputation for great aptitude in the kitchen? What access was there to the correct ingredients? Did a kitchen possess anything more than a primitive stove and rudimentary equipment? The cooks, in their turn, probably railed against the perceived blandness of certain dishes by trying to perk them up with well-tried spices and other techniques.

Thus, dishes such as gypsy roast came into being. This is a roast chicken with a distinctive Calcutta twist or, as Afroze put it, "Your roast is quite bland but ours has more flavor." Here, the chicken is stuffed with minced chicken liver, egg, and bread crumbs, and the whole thing is then cooked in a pressure cooker. The accompanying sauce is made using red onion, meat juices, stock, mustard, Tabasco sauce, whole pepper, and cardamom. In the old days all the Bengal cooks were Mogs and, although they have long since departed, their repertoire remains: all sorts of stuffed fish, steak and kidney pie, glazed hams, roast mutton (here served with mint sauce and guava as opposed to red currant jelly), almond soufflé, and most importantly, that obligatory second course at lunchtime: the omelet.

Although the outlook and thinking of the clubs remains stiffly stratified and there remain strict dress rules enforced by servers and staff still outfitted in seemingly antiquated (and, at times, threadbare) uniforms, the clubs today operate in a vastly different world and cater for a different elite. They were constructed in an era of strict social precedence and snobbery that governed every aspect of life, including food. Under the nom de plume Wyvern, the food writer Colonel Kenney-Herbert published in the late 19th century a series of recipe books including, in 1881, *Sweet Dishes: A Little Treatise*. In it, not only does he go as far as grading puddings into three different classes depending on the costliness of their ingredients, the skill of the cook, and the suitability of the social function, but he ends up reminding his readers (largely the memsahibs of the day) that "caramel pudding is a kind of sweet that, independently of its innate simplicity, generally finds favor with people of refined taste." How heartened he would be to learn that such a dish seems never to leave the pudding repertoire of any Calcutta club worth its salt.

Steamed fish roll in aspic

This fish dish was a centerpiece for banquets in clubs or wealthy households. Traditionally it was very delicately flavored, but its real attraction is its appearance — as a piece of gastronomic genius. It requires quite a lot of skill to highlight the natural flavors of the fish with such simplicity. You should allow ample time to prepare this dish, as it is better made a day in advance.

Serves 8-10

1lb 12oz-2lb 4oz filet of flaky white fish (*bhetki*, cod, or haddock)

4–5 shallots, peeled and sliced

1-inch piece fresh ginger, peeled and cut into matchstick strips

3–4 sprigs fresh mint leaves, torn

3–4 medium dried bay leaves

1 tsp black peppercorns, crushed

2 tsp paprika

½ tsp sugar

about 2 quarts water

Pickled vegetables

2 medium carrots

1 medium *mooli* (white radish)

2½ cups water

3 tsp sugar

2 tbsp malt vinegar

salt

2 medium fresh red chilis, cut into quarters or cut diagonally, seeded

Aspic

4 tbsp agar-agar crystals or 2 tbsp powdered gelatin

1 quart warm water

1 tbsp chopped fresh parsley (optional)

Salad

1 small cabbage

1 green sweet pepper, seeded

juice of 1 lemon

½ tsp fresh ground black pepper

salt

3–4 sprigs fresh parsley

1 Wash the fish in cold water and then set aside. You can skin it if you like, but this is not imperative, and, in fact, with skin on the fish it is easier to transfer to the serving dish once cooked.

2 In a large casserole or similar dish (a fish kettle, say), combine all the other fish ingredients. Bring to a boil, then simmer gently for about 15 minutes with the lid on so the water absorbs all the flavors.

3 Lay the fish carefully in the liquid, bring back to a boil, then reduce to a simmer and cook gently for 12–15 minutes. Check that the fish is cooked — it should readily flake if gently pressed with a fork. Remove the fish from the liquid using a large flat spatula, and place on a decorative serving dish. Allow to cool at room temperature.

4 To make the pickled vegetables, peel the carrots and *mooli*, then carve them whole before slicing so you end up with shaped slices. You could have rounds or squares, but if you let your creative juices flow, you could make fish, birds, rabbits, bells, hearts, etc. Or you could use a suitable vegetable or cookie cutter. Keep the trimmings.

5 Bring the 2¼ cups water to a boil with the sugar and vinegar and some salt to taste. After 3 minutes, remove from heat and add the *mooli* and carrots. Allow this to cool, then remove and drain the vegetables.

6 Arrange the vegetable shapes randomly over the fish, occasionally interspersing them with the chilis.

7 For the aspic, dissolve the agar-agar or gelatin in the warm water, according to the package instructions. Simmer for about 15 minutes to reduce slightly to about 3½ cups. Cool to room temperature. If you like you could add the parsley now, which will give you a green aspic. Ladle a layer of aspic on to the fish, cover, and put in the fridge. Repeat this layering and chilling twice more to get a good coating.

8 To make the salad, cut the carrot and *mooli* trimmings into fine shreds. Shred the cabbage and green pepper. Mix all together in a serving bowl. Make a dressing from the lemon juice, the pepper, and some salt.

9 Trim the aspic from the plate around the fish, remove it and discard. Frame the fish with the fresh salad and garnish with sprigs of parsley.

❖ Fish moilee

Simon gave me this recipe, which comes from Bob Wright's cook, Samir. Known as *moilee* and *mollee*, the dish is Portuguese in influence. The Portuguese had settled in Goa, and local cooks who worked in their kitchens would sail as galley cooks to other parts of India, including Calcutta. Because they were good cooks, a lot of them ended up in British clubs and households in the city.

Serves 4

1lb 12oz skinless filet of white flaky fish (*bhetki*, cod, or haddock)

salt

1 tsp turmeric

vegetable oil

Sauce

1-inch piece fresh ginger, peeled and chopped

4 garlic cloves, peeled and chopped

1 tsp cumin seeds

1 tsp brown mustard seeds

2–3 whole dried red chilis, torn and seeded

3 tsp white poppy seeds

1 tsp turmeric

3–4 sprigs fresh cilantro

about 8–10 curry leaves

2 medium onions, peeled, halved, and sliced

⅛ cup coconut milk

salt

sugar

juice of ½ lemon

1 tsp garam masala (*see* page 21)

1 Cut the fish into 8–10 pieces as desired. Sprinkle with salt to taste and the turmeric. Pan-fry the fish in vegetable oil at high heat, turning over, until light golden in color, about 5 minutes. Drain well and keep warm.

2 For the sauce, blend the ginger, cloves, cumin, mustard seeds, chilis, poppy seeds, turmeric, and cilantro to a smooth paste, using a little water.

3 Heat 2 tbsp of the fish cooking oil in a shallow pan, and add the curry leaves and onion. Cook until the onion is just light gold in color, about 5–7 minutes, and then add the sauce. Fry this well for 5–6 minutes, until you get the aroma of cooked garlic. Add the coconut milk, salt, and sugar to taste, and simmer this for 3–4 minutes. Add about ¼ cup water to get a sauce of medium pouring consistency.

4 Arrange the pieces of fish in the sauce, and simmer for 3–4 minutes. Stir in the lemon juice, and serve sprinkled with garam masala.

❖ Chicken jalfraizee
Stir-fried chicken and peppers

This dish is a classical way of using up a Sunday club roast — so you could have a beef, mutton, lamb, or chicken *jalfraizee*. The recipe found its way into homes from the thrifty kitchens of the Calcutta clubs. *Jal* means "hot" and *fraizee* is a colloquial way of saying "fried".

Serves 4

1 chicken, roasted (*see* page 133), or 4 large raw chicken breasts, skinned and boned

salt

½-inch piece fresh ginger, peeled

2 garlic cloves, peeled

1 tsp turmeric

1 tsp red chili powder

juice of 1 lemon

2 tbsp mustard oil

1 green sweet pepper, seeded and cut into strips

2 medium red onions, peeled and cut into strips

2 large tomatoes, quartered, seeded, and cut into strips

1 tsp garam masala (*see* page 21)

Sauce

¼-inch piece fresh ginger, peeled and roughly chopped

4 garlic cloves, peeled and roughly chopped

2 tbsp vegetable oil

1 tsp cumin seeds

3 medium onions, peeled and finely chopped

1 tsp ground cumin

1 tbsp ground coriander

2 tsp red chili powder

1 tsp turmeric

5 tomatoes, chopped

about 8 sprigs fresh cilantro, chopped

sugar

salt

1 Skin the roast chicken, and take the meat off the bone. Cut the meat into strips. Or cut the boneless raw breasts into strips, and apply some salt.

2 Blend the ginger and garlic together to a paste. Mix the turmeric, red chili powder, and half the lemon juice with the ginger-garlic paste, and rub the mixture into the chicken strips.

3 Heat the mustard oil to smoking, then cool slightly. Add the chicken strips and stir-fry rapidly for 2 minutes, depending on the thickness of the strips. Remove from the pan. In the same hot oil, very rapidly stir-fry the pepper, onion, and tomato. Remove and mix with the chicken. Reserve the oil in the pan.

4 Now begin the sauce. Blend the ginger and garlic to a paste. Add the vegetable oil to the mustard oil in the pan, heat, add the cumin seeds, and allow them to crackle. Add the onion and cook for about 4–5 minutes until it starts darkening, then add the ginger-garlic paste and the ground spices. Cook for about 2½–3 minutes, until you get the aroma of well-fried garlic. Add the tomato and cilantro, then sugar and salt to taste. Cook for 5 minutes.

5 Add the chicken and vegetables to the sauce and mix gently together, adding 2 tbsp water, and cook until the chicken is cooked through, to get a medium-thick consistency — this should take 3–5 minutes.

6 Sprinkle the garam masala and the remaining lemon juice over the top, and serve hot with a *polao* (*see* pages 61 and 176).

◆ Masala shrimp

This is shrimp cooked with tomatoes, chilis, and garlic. Medium-size saltwater shrimp are preferable to large freshwater shrimp and crayfish. This dish would rarely be seen on Bengali tables, but would be a sought-after club delicacy.

Serves 4

2lb 4oz medium shrimp

juice of ½ lemon

salt

1 tsp red chili powder

1 tsp turmeric

3 tbsp vegetable oil

3–4 sprigs fresh cilantro, chopped

Red masala paste

1 tsp cumin seeds

1 tbsp coriander seeds

½ tsp black peppercorns

4 cloves

1-inch cinnamon stick

2 green cardamom pods

1 medium dried bay leaf

6 medium whole dried red chilis, torn and seeded

1-inch piece fresh ginger, peeled and roughly chopped

6 garlic cloves, peeled and roughly chopped

1 small onion, peeled and roughly chopped

1 tsp sugar

1 tsp turmeric

½ tsp salt

2 tbsp malt vinegar

Masala gravy

6 garlic cloves, peeled and sliced

2 medium onions, peeled and finely chopped

4 medium tomatoes, chopped

1 tbsp tomato paste

1 Shell and devein the shrimp. Rub the lemon juice, salt to taste, the red chili powder, and turmeric into the prawns, and leave for a few minutes to marinate.

2 Grind or blend the red masala ingredients to a fine paste, using a little more vinegar instead of adding water, if necessary.

3 To cook the shrimp, heat the oil in a medium-size frying pan, and fry them for 2–3 minutes, until they change color. Remove and drain.

4 Reheat the oil, and add the sliced garlic for the gravy. Cook for 2 minutes, until it just starts darkening. Add the onion, stir and gently cook for 8–10 minutes, until just starting to color. At this point, add the red masala paste and fry for about 3 minutes, stirring continuously. Add the chopped tomatoes, and cook for 4–5 minutes, until they dissolve into the gravy. Mix the tomato paste in well, then add the shrimp and check the salt. The gravy should be a thick coating consistency. If required, add 2 tbsp water.

5 Cook for a few minutes, until the dish is heated through, and serve garnished with chopped cilantro.

Egg curry with yellow split peas

This dish consists of boiled eggs with yellow split peas and was a favorite of the Mogs, who presided over most club kitchens. It is a very thrifty and tasty way of converting any leftover soaked lentils into an interesting and nutritious dish. One would hardly ever see this as part of a main menu, but often it would be good enough to provide a quick meal.

Serves 4

4 medium eggs, hard-boiled and shelled

1 tsp turmeric

1 tsp red chili powder

½ tsp salt

1 tbsp chickpea flour

1 tbsp mustard oil

5–6 sprigs fresh cilantro, chopped

½ tsp garam masala (*see* page 21)

Dal

2½ cups yellow split peas, washed and soaked overnight

1 medium fresh green chili, roughly chopped

1 tbsp vegetable oil

½ tsp brown mustard seeds

1 tsp cumin seeds

1 medium onion, peeled, halved, and sliced

1-inch piece fresh ginger, peeled and chopped

5–6 medium curry leaves, chopped

2 tbsp plain yogurt

2 tsp turmeric

1 tsp red chili powder

about 1 cup water

salt

a pinch of sugar

1 Make 2 scores on the cooked egg white and moisten the eggs slightly with water. Mix the turmeric, red chili powder, salt, and chickpea flour together and use to coat the eggs. Heat the mustard oil until smoking in a *karai* or heavy wok, cool slightly, then fry the eggs for 3–4 minutes, until golden in color. Drain and set aside.

2 Drain off the water from the yellow split peas, rinse, then grind with the green chili and about 3 tbsp water to a coarse texture.

3 Strain the mustard oil used for frying the eggs, and put it in a saucepan. Add the vegetable oil and heat. Add the mustard seeds and allow them to crackle, then add the cumin seeds. When they start to brown, about 30 seconds, add the onion and cook until dark brown, 3–4 minutes. Add the ginger, curry leaves, yogurt, turmeric, and red chili powder, and cook for 2–3 minutes before adding the ground split peas mixture (dal). The split peas will tend to stick, so you must cook gently, and stir continuously for about 10 minutes. After this time, the dal should be coming off the bottom of the pan — a sign that it is cooked. Add the water, sugar, and salt to taste; mix together well and heat through.

4 To serve, cut the fried eggs in half and arrange them in a shallow serving dish. Pour over the thick dal, and serve with chopped cilantro and garam masala sprinkled on top.

❖ Duck dumpode
Baked stuffed duck

This is a duck version of the gypsy chicken Simon mentions in his introduction. You could use any medium-size game bird or livestock poultry, but because the dish is elaborate to prepare it would be reserved for a special bird. The ingredients suit the strong gamey flavors of geese. *Dumpode* originates from *dum-in phukt*, which comes from the Nawabi style of cooking meats sealed in hot vessels.

Serves 4

3lb 5oz duck, with giblets
½-inch piece fresh ginger
2 garlic cloves
coarse-grained salt
5 tsp turmeric
2 tsp red chili powder
2 tbsp all-purpose flour
vegetable oil
3 medium carrots, peeled
8 small potatoes
3 small turnips, peeled and quartered
4¼ cups all-purpose flour

Stuffing

1½-inch piece fresh ginger
1lb 2oz lean ground beef
2 potatoes, peeled and finely diced
2 medium onions, peeled and chopped
6–8 garlic cloves, peeled and chopped
1 tsp ground cumin
3 tsp red chili powder
2 tsp garam masala (*see* page 21)
2 tbsp ghee
1 cup dried white breadcrumbs soaked in about ¼ cup milk
½ cup currants

Sauce

1⅛ cups plain yogurt
a few saffron strands
2 tsp red chili powder
1 tsp turmeric
1 tbsp all-purpose flour
salt
sugar
3 garlic cloves, peeled and chopped
3 tbsp red wine
Crisp fried onions, recipe doubled (*see* page 61), chopped
3 tbsp heavy cream

1 Wash and dry the duck. Peel and chop the ginger and garlic and blend it into a paste in a mortar and pestle. Rub the duck with the ginger-garlic paste, the coarse-grained salt, 3 tsp of turmeric, the red chili powder and the 2 tbsp all-purpose flour. Heat 3 tbsp of vegetable oil in a *karai* or large wok to medium-hot, and brown the duck on all sides. Drain and set aside. Retain the oil for the vegetables.

2 For the stuffing, peel and finely chop the ginger. Chop the duck giblets and mix with the ground beef and all the other stuffing ingredients up to and including the ghee, plus 1 tsp turmeric. Put this in a *karai* or large wok and cook over low heat for about 40 minutes. Mash the mixture with a potato masher, adding the breadcrumbs. Add the currants, let cool, then stuff the duck. Place the duck in a large, deep casserole dish.

3 Preheat the oven to 375°F. Cut the carrots into 1-inch chunks. Parboil the potatoes whole, skin on. Stir-fry the carrots, potatoes, and turnips quickly in the same oil as the duck. Strain the oil into a saucepan.

4 For the sauce, mix the yogurt with the spices, the all-purpose flour, plus salt and sugar to taste. Set aside.

5 Heat the duck oil in the pan, adding more if necessary. Add the garlic and fry until brown. Add the red wine and boil to reduce almost completely. Add the crisp fried onions. After 30 seconds, add the yogurt mixture and cook for 5–10 minutes. You need a pouring consistency, so you might need to add water, about ½ cup at a time, until it is right. Add the cream and heat until warm. Add more water if needed.

6 Pour this sauce over the duck in the casserole dish, and cover with the lid. Roast in the oven for about 2 hours, basting with the sauce every ½ hour.

7 Remove the casserole dish from the oven and arrange the vegetables around the duck. Baste again, and check consistency and seasoning.

8 Mix the 4¼ cups all-purpose flour with enough water to make a firm but pliable dough. Roll this into a rope, which you place around the lip of the casserole dish. Moisten the edges of the lid, and press it down on to the dough. Return the sealed dish to the oven for another 40 minutes.

8 Open the casserole at the table. The meat should be coming off the bone. Serve with the vegetables and gravy and a *polao* (*see* pages 61 and 176).

❖ Country captain
Mild chicken curry with saffron

The "country captain" could be described as an adapted style of korma, suitable for people not accustomed to spices. The name may have come from dishes prepared for officers of the Raj when they were "out in the country," *i.e.* away from the confines of their garrisons and clubs, and the normal brigade of cooks was not with them. This became so popular that it started to appear on club menus.

Serves 4

2lb 4oz chicken

2 tsp turmeric

salt

3 medium onions, peeled and cut into big chunks

1 cup broken cashew nuts (available in packets)

about 2¼ cups water

1-inch piece fresh ginger, peeled and roughly chopped

6 garlic cloves, peeled and roughly chopped

2 tbsp vegetable oil

1 tsp cumin seeds

2 medium dried bay leaves

Crisp fried onions, (*see* page 61), half recipe

1 tbsp ground coriander

2 tbsp heavy cream

a good pinch of saffron strands

1 tsp paprika

2 sprigs fresh mint, chopped

3–4 sprigs fresh cilantro, chopped

1 tsp garam masala (*see* page 21)

Garnish

1 tbsp ghee

1 large tomato, seeded and cut into strips

2 medium fresh green chilis, cut and seeded (according to taste)

1 Skin the chicken and cut into about 10 pieces: each breast into 2 and each leg into 3. Coat the chicken pieces with 1 tsp turmeric, add salt to taste, and set aside.

2 Boil the onions and cashew nuts in the water for 15–20 minutes, until the onions are soft. Blend to a smooth paste. Separately, grind the ginger and garlic together to a paste.

3 Heat the vegetable oil in a deep saucepan and add the cumin seeds. Allow them to crackle, then add the bay leaves. Add the crisp fried onions and the ginger-garlic paste, and cook until you get the aroma of cooked garlic. Add the ground coriander and remaining turmeric and cook for 2 minutes, then add the boiled onion-cashew paste. Bring this to a simmer, add the chicken pieces, and cook fairly gently for about 20 minutes, turning the chicken, until it is cooked through. Add the cream, saffron, paprika, mint, and cilantro, salt to taste, and the garam masala, and cook for another 2–3 minutes to heat through. The consistency should be medium-thick. Put in a serving dish.

4 To finish the dish, heat the ghee in a small frying pan, and rapidly fry the tomato and green chilis. Pour over the curry and serve with some boiled rice.

Echoes of a colonial past. Left, clockwise from top: the Victoria Memorial, the General Post Office, and a statue of David Hare, educationalist and a founder of what became Presidency College. Right: a server at the Bengal Club.

❖ Mulligatawny
Spicy lentil soup

Mulligatawny is one of the best-known Indian soups from the days of the Raj, and it would have appeared on every club menu. It is almost synonymous with south Indian curry pastes. It is a combination of lentils and spices, cooked to a smooth and peppery finish (the name in Tamil means "pepper water": *mulli* is pepper, and *tanni* is water). Officers of a club would vie to serve the most peppery soup.

Serves 4

1 tbsp vegetable oil

3–4 shallots, peeled and chopped

1 cup plus 3 tbsp red lentils

2-inch piece fresh ginger, peeled and chopped

6–8 curry leaves

2 medium fresh green chilis, chopped

8–10 black peppercorns to taste

1 tbsp Madras curry powder

1 large cooking apple, peeled and diced

1 small potato, peeled and diced

½ tsp garam masala (*see* page 21)

3 tbsp fresh grated coconut (*see* page 159)

salt

sugar

1 quart water

Garnish

4 tbsp boiled rice

1 lemon, cut into 4 wedges

1 Heat the vegetable oil in a medium pan over medium-low heat, add the shallots and fry briefly for about a minute. Add all the other ingredients up to and including the salt and sugar to taste, and fry for another 6 minutes. Add the water, bring to a boil, then cover and simmer for about half an hour.

2 Purée or blend the mixture to a smooth liquid. Adjust seasoning as necessary. Serve hot, with 1 tbsp of rice dropped in each bowl, and a wedge of lemon, to squeeze, per serving.

❖ Pork bhoonie
Fried roast pork

Bhoonie has the same root as *bhuna*, the familiar restaurant term, and it means "twice-cooked." In a restaurant, a meat would be stewed first and then fried; in this dish it is roasted first and then fried. Pork is not usually consumed in Bengali households, but pigs were especially reared for the British to give good meat, and recipes for it were created by the cook.

Serves 4

2lb 4oz lean pork from the rump, trimmed of any fat

Roasting

1-inch piece fresh ginger, peeled and roughly chopped

8 garlic cloves, peeled and roughly chopped

3 medium onions, peeled and roughly chopped

a good pinch of saffron strands

6–8 cloves

1 tbsp coarse-grained salt

2 tsp brown sugar

3 tbsp vegetable oil

Frying

12 sprigs fresh dill, chopped

3 red onions, peeled and cut into thick rings

6 whole dried red chilis, torn and seeded

4 medium fresh green chilis, cut lengthwise

salt

2 tbsp tamarind pulp

1 Preheat the oven to 375°F. Wash and dry the pork. Pierce it in several places with a sharp knife or skewer. Blend the ginger, garlic, and onion to a paste in a mortar and pestle, and rub this over the pork.

2 Heat the saffron, cloves, and coarse-grained salt in a small pan on the stovetop over low heat, then grind them to a fine powder in a mortar and pestle. Rub this and the sugar onto the meat.

3 Heat the vegetable oil in a *karai* or large, heavy wok and seal the meat, browning it evenly on all sides. Remove the meat, reserving the oil, and put it into a deep casserole dish. Cover and cook in the oven for 40 minutes, turning a couple of times.

4 Remove the casserole dish from the oven and put it on the top of the stove. Add the reserved pork frying oil, the dill, onion, dried and fresh chilis, salt to taste, and tamarind. Cook this on a very slow heat on the stovetop, stirring occasionally, until the onion and dill have become really soft and the meat is cooked through — about 15–20 minutes. The meat will be glazed with the sauce.

5 Remove the pork from the dish and slice it thinly. Pour any visible oil out, and spoon the onion sauce over the pork slices. Serve hot with *porothas*.

❖ Salt beef

Beef was difficult to get hold of in British households, because their staff were usually Hindu and beef is a sensitive issue for the Hindus. So beef, which the British prized more than lamb or mutton, became easier to cook and serve in the clubs. Salting beef was purely a way of preserving it in the days before refrigeration.

Serves 4–6

2 tbsp potassium nitrate

juice of 6–8 limes

3 tbsp brown sugar

2lb 4oz rump of beef

2 tbsp coarse-grained salt

1 Heat the potassium nitrate gently over low heat and powder it finely. Mix the potassium nitrate, lime juice, and sugar, and apply this to the meat in a bowl or dish. Poke the meat all over with a fine skewer and sprinkle with the salt. Cover with a clean, moist cloth and leave for 2 days in the fridge. At least twice a day, pierce and turn the meat to allow the juices to come out and the flavors to be absorbed.

2 Put the meat into a casserole dish and put on a very gentle heat on the stovetop, with no oil or water. Cook for about an hour in its own juices, turning occasionally. As the juices dry up, the meat starts to brown. You might need more time to cook it to tender.

3 The meat can then be sliced when required, and used in salads and sandwiches.

TOLLYGUNGE CLUB LTD.
WAHI CUP

1979	R. R. PURI
1980	MR. J. BAIN
1981	MR. RISHI NARAIN
1982	MR. MRS. VIJAI SINGH
1983	MR. & MRS. L. J. TOMPSETT
1984	MR. B. S. RANDHAWA
1985	MR. VIJAI SINGH
1986	MR. SATISH MEHTA
1987	MR. A. L. CHAKRABORTY
1988	MR. B. P. BAJORIA
1989	MR. M. K. PAUL
1990	MRS. J. M. DAS & MR. F. A. GOMES
1991	MRS. U. BHATTACHARYA
1992	MR. R. H. WRIGHT O.B.E
1993	MR. B. P. BAJORIA
1994	MR. S. R. GHOSHDASTIDAR
1995	MR. SHYAMAL BHATTACHARYA
1996	MR. S. KUMAR BASU
1997	MR. HARI DEY
1998	MR. A. K. CHADHA
1999	MR. ABHAS SEN
2000	MR. A. K. NEVATIA

Potato and ground beef rissoles

Aloo keema chop (*see* page 141) is a modern version of these potato and ground beef rissoles. Classically these were very moderately spiced to suit the taste of the British. They would be accompaniments to more elaborate roasts, which were typical of club banquet menus, rather than snacks.

Makes 12

5 medium potatoes, boiled, peeled, and mashed

salt

a pinch of fresh grated nutmeg

¼ tsp black peppercorns, crushed

2 medium eggs, beaten

1½ cups fresh white bread crumbs

vegetable oil

Filling

10½oz lean ground beef

1 medium carrot, peeled and finely chopped

2-inch piece celery stick, finely chopped

2 small onions, peeled and finely chopped

salt

2 tbsp butter

1 Mix the mashed potato with salt to taste, the nutmeg, and peppercorns. Divide the mixture into 12 equal portions and set aside.

2 For the filling, combine the ground beef with the carrot, celery, onion, and salt to taste. Melt the butter in a pan, add the ground beef mixture, and cook on a gentle heat for 18–20 minutes until browned, cooked, and dry.

3 To make the rissoles, form each portion of mash into a ball. Put the ball in the palm of your hand and make a depression in it with your forefinger. Put 1 tbsp of ground beef mixture into this depression and fold the potato over and around it. Form it into a barrel shape. Repeat to make all the rissoles.

4 Dip these into the beaten egg and coat in bread crumbs, pressing them in well. Deep-fry in medium-hot vegetable oil until crisp and golden. Drain well before serving.

❖ Caramel custard

Indian cooks had to learn how to make desserts for the reserved palates of the sahibs and memsahibs. Caramel custard or "pudding" fitted the bill perfectly. It's a baked custard of egg yolks and milk, with a hint of vanilla and the acridity of caramel. In the days of the Raj, it would have been steamed, rather than baked, in a bain-marie in a large wood-fired oven.

Serves 4
⅓ **cup sugar**
1 **quart whole milk**
3 **medium egg yolks**
2–3 **drops vanilla extract**

1 Preheat the oven to 400°F. Add most of the sugar to the milk, reserving about 3 tbsp of sugar. Simmer to melt the sugar, then boil and simmer the milk to reduce by about a quarter, to 3 cups. Cool the milk.

2 Mix the egg yolks with the sweetened cooled milk, and beat together. Add the vanilla extract.

3 Caramelize the reserved sugar in a small saucepan. Remove from heat and carefully add 1 tbsp of water to dilute the caramel. Divide equally among four 3-inch molds, swirling around to wet the sides. Pour in the egg and milk mixture, and place the molds in a bain-marie (or a roasting tray of hot water). Bake in the oven for about 25 minutes, until custard sets.

4 Cool, then unmold each custard onto a serving plate; you might need to gently pull away at the sides. As you invert the custard, the caramel will run over the plate. Serve warm or chilled.

Baked rice pudding

There are no connections between a *payesh* (Bengali rice pudding, *see* page 160) and this baked rice pudding, which is set with egg whites. This is the sort of pudding you would have expected to find on club menus, and it is now familiar on hotel menus. It is always eaten steaming hot from the oven, because it shrinks if left to cool.

Serves 6

⅓ cup broken basmati rice
¼ cup plus 1 tbsp sugar
1 quart whole milk
½ cup shelled cashew nuts
½ cup raisins
2 medium eggs
½ cup heavy cream
2–3 drops vanilla extract
½ cup sliced almonds
superfine sugar

1 Preheat the oven to 375°F. Wash the rice and drain.

2 Dissolve the sugar in the milk over a gentle heat, then bring the milk to a boil. Simmer for 10–12 minutes, scraping the sides as the milk reduces. Add the rice, cashew nuts, and raisins, and keep cooking gently until the rice grains are soft, about 20 minutes. Cool.

3 Whisk the eggs with the cream and vanilla in a separate bowl and then add to the cooled rice. Pour into six 3-inch ovenproof molds. Sprinkle the almonds on top, then bake for 12–15 minutes. Remove and allow to set a little.

4 Dredge the top with superfine sugar and serve hot in the molds.

Banana fritters

Bananas are available in Calcutta all year. They are eaten when they are in their prime, and when slightly overripe they make excellent fritters. The marriage of these fritters and ice cream took place in the clubs; at home, Bengalis would drench them with liquid date-palm jaggery or a sugar syrup. Fruit as a dessert is a Western custom; in India we'd eat puddings or sweetened yogurts.

Serves 4

4 large overripe bananas
½ cup all-purpose flour
2 tbsp rice flour
a pinch of baking soda
¼ tsp fennel seeds, finely ground
water
vegetable oil
superfine sugar
ice cream

1 Peel and cut the bananas in half, then into chunks, handling them carefully. Mix the flours together with the baking soda and ground fennel. Add water to this, a little at a time, to form a smooth paste. Then thin it down further to a batter of medium-thin consistency (it should almost be like a tempura batter).

2 Heat the vegetable oil in a shallow frying pan over medium heat. Dip each piece of banana in the batter, and pan-fry for about 4–5 minutes, turning the fritters over, until crisp and golden. Drain well.

3 Either sprinkle superfine sugar over or serve with ice cream.

মুসলমানী রান্না

MUSLIM COOKING

At a friend's house, set back on Lower Circular Road, I met a determined, self-confident girl called Pia, who'd grown up in a conservative, strict Hindu household. She related how she was expected to serve her father and brothers at the table and was once admonished by her mother for asking one brother whether he wanted more rice. "You don't ask a man whether he wants to eat or not; you just serve him and it's his prerogative to waste it," she was told. Her only contact with Muslims was the fruit vendors who came to the house and a driver in the household. It was unthinkable that she or her sisters would look at a Muslim boy. All her older sisters had arranged marriages, but Pia fell in love with a Muslim — and one from an enlightened family — whom she married.

In a story of twists and turns, Pia talked about how no one knew of this clandestine affair right up until the day of the marriage — and of how she left her family home never to return, only to end that same day eating biryani and *zarda* (sweet rice) in the house of her new in-laws. Her diet changed completely overnight: more meat, less fish. She'd never eaten beef before. Combinations changed, too: lentils and meat, meat and papaya, all were cooked together. And shrimp were turned into a *chingri dopiaza*, heavy with onion and garlic — things that would never be contemplated in a Hindu Bengali kitchen. So, same city, different religions, and utterly different ways of cooking.

On June 23, 1757, the Battle of Plassey took place far to the north of Calcutta. Here, under Robert Clive, British forces defeated the Nawab of Murshidabad, Siraj-ud-Daula, and Moghul rule of Bengal was effectively brought to an end. But the influence of the Moghuls is still tangible. Under emperor Akbar, who ruled from 1555 and 1605, a courtier Abul Fazl wrote the *Ain-i-Akbari* (Institutions of Akbar). In it, records remain of the order of the day, often in great detail. For instance, mention is made of the chilling of water, "Saltpetre [potassium nitrate] is now used extensively for its cooling properties, and high and low appreciate the benefit of snow and ice brought from the northern mountains."

Abul Fazl also points out the refinements of the cooking at court. Recipes are given, and there are even classes of cooked dishes: meatless, meat cooked with rice, and stand-alone dishes such as the kebab,

dumpukht, and *dopiaza* (a dish needing "twice the amount of onions," which is what the word means in Bengali). Food staples are also listed: grains, legumes, nuts, saffron, and the huge variety of fruit in the markets, from citrus to dried, including pineapples and custard apples.

In Bengal, the court of the Nawabs encompassed many rituals laid down in the *Ain-i-Akbari*. Ice pits were dug to produce sherbets and *kulfi* and gardens were landscaped for the cultivation of roses and the production of *attar*. The vast range of mangoes is a throwback to the orchards of Murshidabad and Malda in north Bengal, many varieties named after such court favorites as Fawzli, Begumphuli, and Himsagar.

In his film *The Chess Players*, Satyajit Ray gives us an inkling of what life in a Moghul court was like: a refined world peopled with figures with exquisite clothes, manners, and palates. While elements of that heady, perfumed world that drifted across from both Lucknow and Hyderabad still linger, this isn't the only strand of Muslim culture that's apparent in Calcutta.

Many Muslims in the city bear all the hallmarks of the life and food culture of east Bengal, which is much more basic and earthy and shaped by different forces and a different geography. While there may be beef in the diet, there'll also be plenty of fish. Gravies and sauces are thinner and more watery than the rich, almond-thickened excesses of Lucknowi food; east Bengali Muslims would pep up a dish only by using chili or turmeric, while turmeric would never be used in the Moghul cookery of Lucknow as it is believed it kills the taste of meat. Is this a cultural difference? I think it might be a more practical one. Turmeric in Bengal is largely valued for its antiseptic qualities, something needed in its hotter, stickier equatorial climate. Not so in the more arid, drier plains where there's less need to preserve food in the same way.

About 20 percent of Calcutta's population is Muslim and there are numerous enclaves and districts across the city, from Metiabruz to Park Circus. The network of lanes and alleys in the center behind the Grand Hotel fascinate me — here is where Nizam's kebab shop and restaurant used to be and you'll find treats from the yogurt-rich mutton *rezala*, finely ground *shami* kebabs, fragrant biryanis, and flaky *parathas* to the smooth, sweet *firni*. These are all dishes

Paya
Lamb trotter broth

The dish is typical night street food of the Mosque areas of Calcutta. It's usually cooked in large sealed pots overnight and through the day. To thoroughly clean the trotters of the hairs and grime, rub them well with coarse-grained salt and whole wheat flour, then wash this off and sear rapidly over open coals or a gas grill to singe off all the hairs. Wash well again and proceed with the recipe.

Serves 4
12 lambs' trotters

First stage
3 medium onions, peeled and diced
about 8 garlic cloves, peeled
1 bouquet garni (a muslin bag containing 3 cloves, 3 green cardamoms, 2 dried bay leaves, 1 cinnamon stick, 2 black cardamoms, 1 tsp black peppercorns)
2 sprigs mint
5 sprigs cilantro
salt

Second stage
2 tbsp coriander seeds
1 tsp cumin seeds
4–5 dried red chilis, in pieces
1-inch cinnamon stick
1 tsp black peppercorns
3 green cardamoms
3 cloves
2 dried bay leaves
1 small piece mace
½ tsp fennel seed
¼ tsp fenugreek seeds
1 tbsp rice

Third stage
2-inch piece fresh ginger, peeled
10 garlic cloves, peeled
4 tbsp vegetable oil
2 onions, peeled, halved, and sliced
2 tbsp all-purpose flour
2–3 medium fresh green chilis
1 sprig mint
3–4 sprigs cilantro
juice of ½ lemon
a few saffron strands
½ tsp rose water

1 Put all the first-stage ingredients, plus the trotters, into a deep pot and cover with ample water. Bring to a boil, and boil for 5 minutes. Skim off and discard the scum, then cover and simmer gently for about 4 hours. Make sure that the trotters are always submerged by adding more hot water to cover as necessary. After the 4 hours, add some salt to taste.

2 For the second stage, put all the spices and rice in a pan and toast over low heat for about 1½ minutes to dry them a little. Grind in a spice mill to a fine powder. Set aside.

3 Preheat the oven to 325°F.

4 For the third stage, blend the ginger and garlic together into a paste with a little water. Heat the vegetable oil in a deep, large casserole dish on the stovetop, and fry the sliced onion until golden brown. Add the ginger-garlic paste and fry for 2–3 minutes. Add the ground spices and rice from the second stage and fry for a minute, then add the all-purpose flour. Stirring continuously, fry for 2–3 minutes until you get the aroma of cooked flour.

5 Strain the trotters and liquid through a large sieve into the casserole dish with the spices. Add the trotters and discard the rest of the first stage ingredients. Cover the casserole dish and cook in the oven for about 2 hours. Every half hour or so, stir it and add hot water if required. The consistency you need is that of a medium-thick broth. The trotters should be soft to the bone; if not, cook for 20–30 minutes more.

6 Put the pan back on the stovetop over low heat and add the chilis, mint, cilantro, lemon juice, saffron, and rose water. Mix well, check for seasoning, and simmer for 5 minutes to infuse the saffron.

7 Serve with *sheermal* (*see* page 102) or any favorite bread.

Dum ka biryani
Rice with lamb and vegetables

Biryani is up there with the great dishes of the world. It is one of the most glorious uses basmati rice can be put to and is, in effect, the Indian equivalent of risotto. There are as many recipes for biryani as there are cooks, although it is classically prepared with lamb. But where risotto aims for creamy but firm rice, a good biryani should be only barely moist and the rice should be fluffy and the grains separate.

Serves 12

5¼ cups basmati rice

3lb 5oz lamb, ideally from the leg, with some pieces on the bone, cut into 1-inch cubes

1½ cups natural yogurt

1 tbsp ground coriander

1 tbsp red chili powder

2 tsp turmeric

salt

3 tbsp vegetable oil

2-inch piece fresh ginger, peeled and chopped

8 garlic cloves, peeled and finely chopped

2 onions, peeled and sliced

4 tomatoes, cubed

6 green chilis, seeded and thinly sliced lengthwise

1-inch piece fresh ginger, peeled and cut into matchsticks

1 sprig fresh mint, chopped

2 tbsp garam masala (*see* page 21)

½ tsp saffron strands

1 small bunch fresh cilantro, chopped

Crisp fried onions, recipe doubled (*see* page 61)

2 tbsp ghee

1 cup milk

2 cups all-purpose flour

1 Wash the rice in a large bowl. Cover with water, stir, drain, and repeat several times until the water remains clear. Leave covered with water for 30 minutes to allow the grains to swell.

2 Meanwhile, place the lamb in a bowl with the yogurt, ground coriander, red chili powder, turmeric, and a pinch of salt, and allow to marinate for 30 minutes (or you could do this the night before and refrigerate).

3 Heat the vegetable oil in a deep pot with a tight-fitting lid. Blend the chopped ginger and the garlic to a paste in a mortar and pestle. Add the onion to the oil and fry until light brown, about 5 minutes. Stir in the ginger-garlic paste, and fry until the aroma of fried garlic is evident — about 3 minutes. Stir in the lamb pieces with their marinade, then simmer, stirring occasionally, adding enough water to cook the lamb, for about 35–40 minutes. Add the tomatoes, cover and simmer for another 30–35 minutes, stirring occasionally, until the lamb is nearly ready.

4 Remove the pot from the heat and stir in the chilis, the ginger matchsticks, mint, garam masala, half the saffron, half the cilantro and half the crisp fried onions. Cover and set aside.

5 Meanwhile, bring a large pot of water, three times the volume of the rice, to a boil. Add ½ tsp of the ghee, some salt and the drained rice. Cook at a low boil for 4–5 minutes, until half-cooked. Drain, reserving ½ cup of the cooking water.

6 Place the rice on top of the cooked lamb mixture and flavorings. Mix the remaining saffron and milk, and gently warm over low heat. Pour over the rice, then pour on the reserved rice cooking water. Sprinkle with the remaining cilantro and the remaining crisp fried onions.

7 Heat the remaining ghee to smoking point and sizzle it over the rice. Cover with a tight-fitting lid and press a rope of bread dough (made with the flour, a pinch of salt, and enough water to make a firm but pliable dough, *see* baked stuffed duck, page 82), moistening it with more water to ease the process, around the lid to seal it securely.

8 Cook in a preheated oven at 375°F for 18–20 minutes. Open the lid and loosen the rice grains with a flat spoon. To serve, dig to the bottom of the dish to get portions of rice and meat in layers. A classic accompaniment would be a *raita* (seasoned yogurt).

Kakori kabab
Ground lamb kebab

The story goes that the Nawab of Lucknow had lost his teeth, and could not chew. As he dearly loved meat, he commanded his Muslim cooks to make him a dish in which the meat would melt in his mouth. The cooks came up with this outstanding lamb kebab. You will need to have thick, long metal skewers and either a rectangular barbecue or a grill pan that you can balance the skewers on.

Serves 4

1lb 2oz lean lamb from the leg, cubed

1¼oz white lamb fat from the back (the kidneys), cubed

2-inch piece fresh ginger, peeled and chopped

6 garlic cloves, peeled and chopped

½ crisp friend onions recipe (*see* page 61)

1 sprig fresh mint

2–3 sprigs fresh cilantro

½ small green (unripe) papaya, peeled and cubed

⅓ cup roasted yellow split peas

2 tsp red chili powder

½ tsp turmeric

a few saffron strands

a few drops rose water

salt

1 tbsp ghee

Masala

4 green cardamom pods

2 cloves

1-inch cinnamon stick

1 dried bay leaf

½ tsp black peppercorns

1 small piece mace

¼ tsp cumin seeds

¼ tsp fennel seeds

1 Make the masala first. Toast the ingredients in a small pan over low heat to dry them a little, then grind to a fine powder in a spice mill. Set aside.

2 Put the lamb and lamb fat in a large bowl. Blend the ginger and garlic to a paste with the crisp fried onions. Add this to the lamb bowl, with the mint, cilantro, and papaya. Mix and then put in batches into a food processor, blending to a paste. Remove from the food processor and mix with all the other ingredients except the ghee. When everything is mixed well together, add the ghee and mix well again. Chill this mixture, covered, in the refrigerator for about half an hour.

3 Light your barbecue or preheat a broiler to medium heat.

4 Form the meat mixture into 12–16 equal-size balls. Using 12–16 metal skewers, mold the balls along the length of the skewers, about 2 inches long; you might need a little water on your hands. Handle it all gently because the mixture is quite delicate. Chill it again, covered, so that the meat holds on to the skewers; the ghee will solidify and hold it all together.

5 Balance the skewers over the barbecue or broiling pan; they must be suspended so the kebabs aren't touching any metal parts, as the meat would stick straightaway. Grill for 4–5 minutes, turning each skewer once as it cooks. The outside of the kebabs will form a kind of skin when they are cooked; the insides should have the texture of pâté. Serve with *sheermal* (*see* page 102). (Please note that the picture does not show these kebabs.)

tip: Papaya is a tenderizer, whether green or ripe. If you have any green papaya left over, cut the flesh in cubes and freeze for another dish.

Above: *boti kabab*, made with boneless cubes of meat.

⊡ Mutton rost
Roasted leg of lamb

This is a festive Muslim dish, and quite decorative. It would rarely be found outside the home. Usually the lamb would be sliced and adorned with a meat *polao*. The leg of lamb is used off the bone and trimmed of all sinews and fat; get the butcher to do this for you. Either leave in one piece, or get him to separate it into the three groups of muscles. We want the muscle groups to remain intact to avoid shrinkage while roasting. This will ensure the roast is juicy.

Serves 4

1 boned leg of lamb (*see* recipe introduction)

3 medium onions, peeled and diced

2-inch piece fresh ginger, peeled and diced

12 garlic cloves, peeled

½ small papaya, peeled

3 tsp turmeric

1 tbsp red chili powder

2 tsp ground cumin

½ tsp sugar

2 tsp salt

2 tbsp mustard oil

2 tbsp plain yogurt

1 tbsp all-purpose flour

Masala

1 tsp Szechuan pepper

1 tsp black peppercorns

seeds from 1 black cardamom pod

seeds from 5 green cardamom pods

2-inch cinnamon stick

1 tsp fennel seeds

¼ tsp fenugreek seeds

Garnish

1 onion, sliced (as much as desired)

1 lemon, cut into 4 wedges

1 Make the masala first. Toast the ingredients in a small pan over low heat to dry them a little, then grind to a fine powder in a spice mill. Set aside.

2 Put the meat in a roasting tray and prick it here and there with a carving fork. Blend the onion, ginger, garlic, and papaya to a smooth paste. Mix with the turmeric, red chili powder, cumin, sugar, salt, and mustard oil. Rub this all over the meat, and let marinate for about half an hour.

3 Preheat the oven to 375°F.

4 Put about 2–3 tbsp of water in the roasting tray, and bake the meat, uncovered, for 20 minutes. Reduce the oven temperature to 325°F.

5 Remove the tray from the oven and the meat from the tray. Transfer the meat juices to a saucepan and put over medium heat on the stovetop. Add the masala powder. Whisk the yogurt and flour until there are no lumps and add this to the liquid. Bring the mixture to a boil.

6 Return the meat to the roasting tray, and pour the gravy over it. Cover with foil and return to the oven for about 45 minutes. Remove the foil and baste with the juices. Cover again and cook for another 15 minutes. The meat should be tender by this time. If still firm, cook for another 15 minutes, covered. If required, add 1 tbsp or so hot water.

7 Turn the temperature of the oven up to 375°F again, and take the foil off the meat. Bake for 12–15 minutes to brown the top.

8 Slice the meat and serve hot with sliced raw onions, lemon, and a *polao* (*see* page 61).

⊡ Chicken dopiaza
Spicy chicken and onion stir-fry

Chicken *dopiaza* literally means a double stir-fry of chicken with onions: *do* is "two", and *piaza* is "pertaining to onions." Usually in Bengali food, we would first fry the ingredients and then add the liquids; the Bengali Muslims reverse the process in this dish by boiling first and then frying. The main flavor of the dish is well-cooked onions, which is typical of Muslim cooking.

Serves 4

3 tbsp coriander seeds

1 tsp black peppercorns

2 tsp cumin seeds

1lb 12oz boneless chicken pieces, skinned and cubed

3–4 medium onions, peeled and diced

6 garlic cloves, peeled and chopped

1¼-inch piece fresh ginger, peeled and sliced

2⅞ cups natural yogurt

2 tsp turmeric

3 cloves

1-inch cinnamon stick

seeds from 2 black cardamom pods

10 dried red chilis, torn into pieces

2 dried bay leaves

1 tsp salt

6 tbsp ghee

1 Toast the coriander seeds, black peppercorns, and cumin seeds in a small frying pan over low heat until they start to pop and you can smell their aromas. Coarsely grind them in a spice mill.

2 Mix the ground spices with all the remaining ingredients except for the ghee. Leave for half an hour to marinate. (If using lamb or beef instead of chicken, leave to marinate for at least 2 hours.)

3 Put the marinated ingredients into a deep, heavy-bottomed saucepan. Bring to a boil, then simmer for 15 minutes, stirring occasionally. Bring to a boil again, and allow any excess liquid to boil off, leaving the gravy at a coating consistency.

4 Add the ghee to the saucepan and, once the mixture starts frying, stir continuously and allow the masala to brown. Ensure the chicken is cooked through. Spoon off any excess ghee and serve hot with boiled rice or *porothas* (*see* page 152).

Sheermal
Rich baked bread

The sweetness of this bread complements the hot Muslim curries. *Sheermal* was traditionally made in metal tandoor ovens, and was usually made communally. Even now in parts of the Punjab and Pakistan, bread is not baked at home: the women make and knead the dough at home, then go to the village tandoor at night to bake the bread — and to gossip. With modern domestic ovens, it is possible to make these at home.

Makes 12

8½ cups all-purpose flour

½ cup plus 3 tbsp semolina

1 tbsp sugar

a pinch of salt

1 tsp baking powder

½ tsp ground fennel

½ tsp ground cardamom

3 tbsp ghee

1¼ cups milk

1 tbsp heavy cream

1 Sift the all-purpose flour into a bowl, then add the semolina, sugar, salt, baking powder, and the ground spices. Mix well with your fingertips.

2 Add 2 tbsp of the ghee and mix until the texture is like coarse breadcrumbs. Sprinkle in the milk gradually, and knead the mixture thoroughly. The milk is not enough to make it come together as a dough.

3 To form the dough, mix in 1–2 tbsp hot water; the dough should now be soft but firm. Mix in the cream, then let the dough rest for about 20 minutes.

4 Preheat the oven to 400°F, and preheat the grill to medium. Put a baking sheet into the oven to heat up.

5 Form the dough into 12 balls. Chill these for about 10 minutes.

6 Roll 4 of the dough balls to rounds of about 2 inches thick, more like biscuits than bread. Prick all over with a fork, and then place on the hot baking sheet. Bake for about 10–12 minutes. Remove and glaze the tops, using a brush, with some of the remaining ghee. Grill for about 45 seconds, then serve.

7 Make the remaining breads in the same way.

Firni
Rice pudding

This Muslim rice pudding is made at home on a regular basis, and for special occasions such as *Eid*. Traditionally, *firni* is set in washed clay pots, which gives it a wonderfully earthy flavor.

Serves 4

3 cups basmati rice, washed

2 quarts whole milk

1 cup sugar

2 tbsp shelled cashew nuts, roughly chopped

⅝ cup light cream

a few drops rose water

¼ tsp ground cardamom

1 Wash the rice and drain it well. Dry it partially on absorbent paper towels, then grind it in a blender briefly just to break the grains; you don't want a powder.

2 In a deep saucepan, mix the milk and sugar and bring it to a boil. Reduce the heat and simmer, stirring continuously, until reduced by about a quarter. Add the rice and nuts and continue cooking and reducing. Keep scraping the milk from the sides of the pan, this gives the dish its creaminess. Taste to see if it is sweet enough; if not, add more sugar.

3 When the rice is very soft and the texture is quite thick, add the cream, rose water, and cardamom. Mix in well, pour into individual serving bowls, cool, and then chill. A nice creamy skin will form on the top.

4 Serve cold — at any time of the day!

আন্তর্জাতিক কলকাতা

COSMOPOLITAN
CALCUTTA

Crossing the Meccano-like silver structure of Howrah Bridge provokes mixed emotions. For one thing, the traffic's usually hellish — stop-go, stop-go. Then again, for many Calcuttans, this giant, towering matrix of girders and engineering acts as a talisman, welcoming them back to everything that is home and familiar. The bridge leads onto a great curving overpass that sweeps down into one of the most crowded areas of the city: Burra Bazar. It's like a street scene from *Blade Runner* minus the technological futurism: dense, intense human activity. It turns into Brabourne Road, which, once you get beyond the high, overcrowded tenements that flag either side of the street, offers up some fascinating threads of Calcutta life that are important but rapidly fading from view: its cosmopolitan strengths or, if some are to be believed, its cosmopolitan past.

The clues littering Brabourne Road center on a cluster of places of worship. There's the Roman Catholic Church, built in 1950 on the site of a previous church that was erected in 1710, on what was then known as Portuguese Church Street. Across the way, behind thick gates, is the Armenian Church of Nazareth, built in 1724. Tucked off the road is the Shield of David Jewish Synagogue (referred to by Bengalis as the Yehuda Church).

There's the Nakhoda Mosque farther down, and then, just as Brabourne Road reaches the Writers' Buildings, the tall spire of St. Andrew's Kirk stands guard at the entrance into Binay-Badal-Dinesh Bagh (or Dalhousie Square, as it was). Each a focal point for a different community, and each a community that made its way here via a different route and under different circumstances, bringing dishes and ingredients and cooking methods that have, to a greater or lesser extent, become enmeshed within the fabric of Calcutta.

The entrance to the Church of Nazareth is actually on a narrow cobbled alley, Armenian Street. Imposing double doors, made from Burma teak and polished brass, lead into a comparatively hushed courtyard lined with graves that bear names such as Arratoon Apcar, Chater, Stephen, and Galstaun. It's reckoned that the Armenians predate the British — their church is the earliest Christian one here — and many of the earliest settlers were merchants trading in spices and gemstones.

A great wave of migrants left Persia (Iran) after the Turkish massacre of 1917, including the grandfather of a woman called Sonia John who, today, is pivotal in the community, at both its church and the Armenian College. Her grandfather came to Calcutta from Shiraz and went into the shellac business. There's also Violet Smith, who, for many years, has run the Fairlawn Hotel in Sudder Street. She was born in Dhaka after her parents arrived there from Isfahan. Sitting in the small garden at the Fairlawn, our voices almost drowned out by the crows and car horns outside, she told me how the Armenians always worked for themselves. They were enterprising and developed large properties in the Chowringhee and Park Street areas, including some of the great mansion buildings. Arathoon Stephen, another Armenian, built the Grand Hotel (now Oberoi Grand) on the site of the old Theatre Royal. And Violet Smith's mother ended up with a small cluster of boarding houses and hotels, acquiring the Fairlawn (from two old Scottish ladies), as well as the Biltmore, the Astoria, and an establishment at 3 Wood Street.

According to Sonia John, obtaining ingredients in Calcutta was never a problem. Dried fruits and nuts, cherries and saffron, which were fundamental to the diet in Iran, could as easily be sourced from Kabul or Kashmir. The fish most prized by Armenians, the sturgeon, was sent in dried and salted form before it became impossible to obtain. Afterward, the Bengali favorite, *hilsa*, turned out to be the perfect alternative. Every Armenian house grew a grape vine, not so much for its grapes, but more for the leaves to make *dolmas* (stuffed grape leaves), although today, most people have substituted cabbage leaves. And for the Armenians, Christmas (which is in early January) dishes such as *kuku polao* would be produced and still are. The *kuku* is a light, spongy herb omelet (made with cilantro or dill) and is served with fragrant *polao* rice. Other dishes included *pharinj*, a winter dish of broken wheat with braised mutton, and a soup called *chorathan* (*chora*: "dry"; *than*: "curd"). This soup was also eaten mainly in winter and consisted of dried curd made into pellets that were then ground into a soft flour. It was made into soup by adding melted butter and fried onions.

Intertwined with the Armenians were the Jews, although their arrival in the city was much later and can be pinpointed down to one man, Shalom Cohen, who came from Aleppo in Syria in the late 1790s via Surat. I learnt his tale from Ian Zachariah, an ex-advertising executive and food journalist. Ian explained that it's said that Shalom Cohen travelled with a group of servants, even including a *shohet* (someone to perform the ritual slaughter of meat correct for a kosher kitchen). Those who followed after him came largely from Iraq and were known as Baghdadis. They, like the Armenians, were merchants and traders and their descendents, too, dealt in real estate. Many of the more orthodox families kept strict kosher kitchens in which it wasn't acceptable to mix the cooking of milk products with meat — so no yogurt, but coconut milk might be used instead. Many of them had Muslim cooks who came from the town of Midnapore, and who, with little sense of irony, earned themselves the label "Jewish cooks."

There were many common elements between Indian food and what the Baghdadis ate: the use of rice, *brinjal* (eggplant), *bhindi* (okra), nuts, pomegranates, and certain spices. One of the best-known dishes from the Jewish kitchen (and one not brought from the Middle East) is *aloo makallah*, potato coated in turmeric, then deep-fried until crisp on the outside and soft in the middle. This is invariably served with a Jewish chicken roast that is heavily browned in a pressure cooker until it sticks to the pan ("the best bits" according to Ian). *Mahashas*, or stuffed vegetables, are another favorite that use anything in season suited to being scooped out and filled.

Ian and I talked at the Outram Club, certainly not one of the city's premier social establishments. The main bar had all the charm of an executive lounge belonging to a failing airline, so we talked outside on the veranda, where we were given tea and tired chicken sandwiches by a server with a highly distracting cell phone ringtone. As the light faded, his ringtone jarred against the sound of the many muezzins' call to prayer from nearby Park Circus, with its numerous mosques — a cultural mash-up of noises and sounds that often gives Calcutta a poignancy. Ringtone, Allah Akbar, crows, car horns, a snatch of Hindi film music: All layered together in a poetic soundtrack that life in England or the United States doesn't quite prepare you for.

For me, the most visible Jewish presence in Calcutta today is that of the baker and confectioner, Nahoum & Sons, in New Market. I can't remember who took me there first, but I knew the world was a better place when I first tried one of their lemon sponges with its tart, zesty, curd-like filling. David Nahoum, an engineer by trade, took over the family business when his brother Norman died in 1999 and sits, just like Norman did, behind the shop's antique National Cash Register desk with its mild air of Dickensian reprimand. Like so many others, David's grandfather came from Baghdad in 1870 and started making foods specifically for the Jewish community — date babas, baklava, almond samosas, and cheese *samooksas*. He started off in the front of the market (where the flower sellers are today), then moved to the current premises in 1916. Not a lot has changed since then. There's still the Italian zinc paneling and the fine display cases that were crafted by Chinese carpenters out of Burma teak. But now, probably no more than a tiny fraction of what is baked is of Jewish origin.

According to David, there was always a market for English-style things, especially their rich plum cake that even today is popular at Christmas. There used to be an entire team employed to decorate wedding and birthday cakes destined for far-flung corners of eastern India, "although here we use cashew nuts for the marzipan, not almonds." They even made a 45-pound cake in the shape of a train engine for the inauguration of the Chittaranjan Locomotive Works. But then, with the influence of the Swiss and the Italians (at establishments such as Flury's and Firpo's), came the more sugary, spongy confections that you'll find both here and in many other pastry shops across town. Bengalis love sweets, and when they're not eating Bengali sweets, they aim straight for frothy items with frosting, piping, and chocolate dripping from every corner. As elsewhere, Nahoum's makes these in abundance.

Far more visible than either the Jews or the Armenians are the Chinese. They've maintained a strong presence for well over 200 years and have left behind several legacies: a strong tannery industry, rickshaws, and restaurants. Calcuttans adore the version of Chinese cooking that has proliferated across the city in various formats: smart outlets in five-

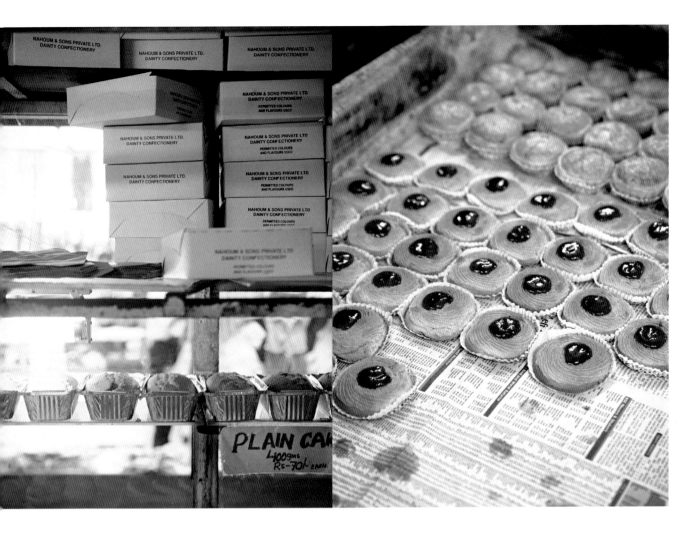

star hotels, upscale restaurants such as Mainland China, and smaller neighborhood places such as Golden Chopsticks in Gariahat, which was a regular haunt of mine. And then there are the endless noodle and chow mein vendors on the street, knocking up platefuls from smoking woks in seconds flat. Thanks to the first Chinese settler — one Yong Atchew, who arrived in 1780 and ended up being buried a few years later in the village of Achipur (named after him) — Calcutta had the first Chinatown outside China centered on Sun Yat Sen Street (formerly Chinabazar Street). Although a delight to many, Sun Yat Sen Street, tucked in next to the business district, has limited charms. Around breakfast time, you'll see people (and fewer of them Chinese as time goes on) selling dumplings, both fish and pork, Tibetan momos, sticky rice cakes, Chinese sausage, and sometimes, in the build-up to a festival such as Chinese New Year, lurid red rice cakes.

More dynamic is Tangra, an area away from the city center near the eastern bypass. You'll know when you're nearly there by the acrid smell of the many tanneries that make up this slightly forbidding world, with its high factory walls and gates somewhat comically interspersed with the neon glow of restaurant doorways. Two of these eateries, Beijing and Kimling, are owned by Monica Liu, who told me that the Chinese here are highly clannish. Those originally from Shanghai do dry-cleaning, the Cantonese have always been carpenters and dentists, while the Hakka people have gone in for tanning and shoemaking. Tangra developed specifically as a tannery zone; the restaurants came much later, but now pull in a sizeable Bengali audience for noodles, steamed fish with scallions, and chili chicken.

In 1962, during the Sino-Indian War, Monica Liu and her family were sent from their home in Shillong (in the north eastern state of Meghalaya) to a detention camp in Rajasthan for five years along with 30,000 other Chinese from across the country. Once the war was over and they were released, she

claims that more than 75 percent left India for Canada, the United States, and Australia. Sitting beside Monica Liu at a smart table in her spacious Park Street restaurant, Tung Fong, I asked her why she didn't leave. Her parents spoke no English or Hindi, she replied, and they couldn't afford to go anywhere. But this thread of certain communities moving on is replicated elsewhere.

Ian Zachariah reckoned that the Jewish population was at its height during World War II, when many fled to Calcutta from Shanghai and Rangoon. But now, most have gone too, again to North American, Great Britain, and Israel. The Armenians aren't much different — they're now a small group clustered around their church and college.

Tibetans also came to Calcutta, and some started a row of tiny places near Elgin Road in Bhowanipore, serving steamed, meat-filled dumplings, or *momos,* and a thick noodle and vegetable soup, sometimes with meat, called *thupka.* These almost-restaurants in Suburban Hospital Road are still there, but trying to find a Tibetan working in one is nearly impossible. David Nahoum said that the number of Jews in Calcutta is "30, plus or minus five" and chuckled. He has three nephews, all born abroad, none of whom want to be bakers in Calcutta. So what does that mean? "Well, the end of the road is not that far off. I'm 79."

And so it goes on. The ebb and flow of people into and out of Calcutta never stops. People arrive daily from the neighboring states of Bihar, Orissa, and Uttar Pradesh, but few, if any, from the longer, more tangled routes leading from Lhasa or Isfahan or Baghdad. There are of course always unexpected arrivals. A highly enterprising Italian woman called Anna Maria has opened the doors of her pizzeria on Middleton Row, in what was the old British Airways office. Bengalis, you see, love pizza and pasta as well. But the general feeling is that Calcutta's cosmopolitan Golden Era has come and gone, and that the shutters are going down rather than coming up.

Mahasas
Stuffed vegetables

This recipe is found in quite a few countries in the Middle East, and was brought to Calcutta by the Baghdadi Jews. It offers a way of stuffing leaves or vegetables with rice and meats (usually lamb or chicken), and is good as a light appetizer served at room temperature or a hot accompaniment to roasted meat during feasts. The vegetables are colorful, and can include tomatoes, peppers, grape leaves, baby eggplants, cucumbers, and red onions.

Serves 4

4 each of 3 vegetables, such as tomatoes, medium green peppers, and grape leaves (*see* recipe introduction)

Filling

2 medium boneless chicken breasts, skinned

½-inch piece fresh ginger, peeled and chopped

3 garlic cloves, peeled and chopped

2 sprigs fresh mint

1 tbsp black peppercorns, crushed

juice of ½ lemon

½ tsp turmeric

½ tsp sugar

salt

1½ cups long-grain rice

1 tbsp vegetable or olive oil

1 tbsp tamarind pulp, diluted in 1 tbsp warm water

½ tbsp olive oil

1 Preheat the oven to 350°F.

2 Cut the tops off the tomatoes and peppers. Using a sharp small knife, remove the insides. Rinse the grape leaves in warm water.

3 For the filling, cut the chicken into cubes and coarsely chop in a food processor with the ginger, garlic, and mint. Add the peppercorns, lemon juice, turmeric, sugar, and a pinch of salt.

4 Parboil the rice in salted water to cover, about 10–12 minutes. Drain and cool. Combine with the chicken mixture and the vegetable or olive oil (use the latter if serving at room temperature).

5 Spoon some filling into the tomatoes and peppers, not too tight as the rice will continue cooking and swelling. Put 1 tbsp of the filling on each of the grape leaves, fold in the edges and roll into croquette shapes, not too tight. Place on an appropriately sized baking tray, seam-side down, and add the tomatoes and peppers. Mix with the tamarind, ½ tbsp olive oil, and a pinch each of sugar and salt, and pour into the tray with the vegetables.

6 Cover with foil and bake for 12–15 minutes, until the chicken is cooked through. Remove the foil and cook for another 8–10 minutes. Baste with a little of the tamarind pulp.

Aloo makallah
Crusty potatoes

These potatoes serve as an accompaniment to almost every Jewish meal. You can never make enough of them, so when cooking, plan on at least 4–5 per person. Ideally, use small potatoes and cook them whole; but if you use large ones, cut them in half or into quarters. Try not to use new potatoes, as you need a bit of starch.

Serves 4

16–20 small potatoes

1 tbsp turmeric

salt

vegetable oil

1 Peel the potatoes and place in a pot with cold water to cover. Add the turmeric and salt to taste, and parboil for about 8–10 minutes. Drain, dry, and pierce at random with the tines of a fork.

2 Place the potatoes in a *karai* or heavy wok, cover with vegetable oil, then bring to a boil. Turn the heat down and simmer gently, moving the potatoes around, for about 20 minutes. At this point, the potatoes can be removed and kept until almost ready to serve, if you wish.

3 Simmer for another 8–10 minutes. Once the potatoes start turning light gold, turn up the heat slightly and fry until they are a darker gold and crisp on the outside.

4 Drain well and serve immediately.

Sama pulao
Aromatic rice with dill

The Bengalis would call this *polao*, but the Armenians call it *pulao* (and in fact, the word is spelt differently everywhere — *pullao*, *pilau*, *pillau* — and it comes from the same root as *pilaff* or *pilav*). This recipe is particularly aromatic in Bengal as we usually use a small-grained, Middle Eastern rice that is sun-dried. You can use basmati instead, but do not wash it, as the starch is needed.

Serves 4

5–6 tbsp vegetable oil

4½ cups short-grain white rice

¼ cup chopped fresh dill

salt

1 Preheat the oven to 350°F.

2 Heat the vegetable oil in a deep, heavy-bottomed ovenproof dish with a tight-fitting lid on the stovetop over medium-low heat. Add the rice and fry for 3–4 minutes, then carefully add the dill, salt to taste, and enough hot water to cover the rice by 1 inch. Bring to a boil, then reduce the heat and cover with the lid. Cook until the water has almost evaporated, about 12–15 minutes, then finish cooking, still covered, in the oven for about 20 minutes.

3 Loosen and aerate the rice with a spatula, and serve hot. Any leftover rice can be cooked and used with meat, or for stuffing vegetables and leaves (*see* page 109).

Kuku
Spicy spinach and herb omelet

This is an Armenian dish, normally eaten as a precursor to a meal, or as a late-morning light meal and served with crusty Armenian bread. This bread is a bit like ciabatta or country rolls, with a crust created by wood-fired ovens (there are quite a few wood-fired Armenian bakeries in Calcutta).

Serves 4

2 cups fresh spinach leaves

½ cup fresh cilantro

6 scallions with green stalks

1½ tsp salt

8 medium eggs

¼ tsp baking powder

1 tsp Madras curry powder

1 tbsp all-purpose flour

1 tbsp vegetable oil

1 Wash, drain well, and chop the spinach, cilantro, and scallions. Sprinkle with the salt and leave for an hour. Gently squeeze out as much liquid as possible, using your hands (you don't want to break up the leaves too much).

2 Beat the eggs in a large bowl, and add the greens, baking powder, curry powder, and all-purpose flour. Mix well.

3 Heat the vegetable oil in a large omelet pan and pour in the egg mixture. Scramble it lightly, then allow it to set, covered with a dinner plate, for about 2 minutes. The top should set fully.

4 The omelet can be folded over and then sliced, or left whole and cut into wedges or quarters.

Khow suey
Noodles with a Burmese coconut curry

This Burmese dish was traditionally used to feed a group. The dish came about when the wife of one of the Burmese generals garrisoned in Calcutta was entertaining. She served one of her national curries, but with Asian noodles. Lamb, beef, or chicken can be used, but with chicken the recipe is simpler: we don't use the ground spices as below, but add 1 tbsp shrimp paste to the curry instead.

Serves 8

24oz medium egg noodles

Coconut curry

1 tsp coriander seeds

1 tsp cumin seeds

1 tsp fennel seeds

⅓ tsp fenugreek seeds

4 whole dried red chilis

2 medium onions, peeled and coarsely chopped

1-inch piece fresh ginger, peeled

6 garlic cloves, peeled

2 tbsp vegetable oil

2lb 4oz boneless red meat, in ½-inch cubes

1 tsp turmeric

14oz can coconut milk

a pinch of powdered mace

salt

1 tsp garam masala (*see* page 21)

Garnishes

6 sprigs fresh cilantro, chopped

3 scallions, chopped

6–8 fresh green chilis, chopped

3 tbsp crisp fried onions (*see* page 61)

2 hard-boiled eggs, shelled and finely chopped

2¼oz medium egg noodles

vegetable oil

4 garlic cloves, peeled and sliced

2 lemons, cut into wedges

Garnish sauce

3 medium fresh green chilis

2 tbsp dried shrimp paste

1 Make the curry first. Put the seeds and chilis in a frying pan over low heat and toast until the seeds pop and you can smell the aromas of the spices. Grind finely in a spice mill and set aside. Put the onions in the food processor and blend to a paste. Put on a plate. Add the ginger and garlic to the food processor and blend to a paste.

2 Heat the 2 tbsp vegetable oil in a *karai* or heavy wok, and brown the meat cubes. Remove using a slotted spoon and set aside. Fry the ginger-garlic paste in the same oil until you can smell the garlic. Add the onion paste, turmeric, and ground spices. Fry well for 10–12 minutes, then add the meat cubes and about ½ cup water. Bring to a boil, cover, and simmer until the meat is soft (this could be about 15–30 minutes, the lamb taking longer).

3 Add the coconut milk, mace, garam masala, and salt to taste. Mix, heat thoroughly, and leave the curry to one side.

4 Prepare the garnishes, putting them in small dishes. Deep-fry the noodles by first heating vegetable oil for deep-frying. Put a nest of the noodles in your deep-frying basket (or a metal sieve). Dip into the hot oil, and deep-fry, loosening the strands with a fork, until golden and crisp. Drain very well on absorbent paper towel — the noodles will darken as they cool. Use the same oil to deep-fry the garlic, using the sieve rather than the basket. Fry until golden and crisp, then drain very well. This flavored oil can be reserved and used in other cooking.

5 For the sauce, blend the ingredients together with 1 tbsp of the reserved garlic-flavored oil in a food processor, and then serve in small dishes.

6 Boil the noodles per the package instructions, and drain well.

7 To assemble the dish, serve the curry, fried noodles, and garnishes separately on the table, and allow each person to mix and match to taste.

Momos
Nepalese steamed dumplings

These can be made from meat or vegetables. They can be an appetizer or an anytime snack, but are served principally as a breakfast dish in Tibet. Serve with chutney.

Makes about 40 small dumplings (to serve 5–10)

4 cups all-purpose flour

salt

2 raw chickens

Filling

14oz pork or beef with a bit of fat

1 medium onion, peeled and roughly chopped

3–4 garlic cloves, peeled and chopped

3 sprigs fresh cilantro, chopped

salt, to taste

Tomato chutney

4 large red tomatoes

1 tsp red chili powder

5–6 garlic cloves, peeled and chopped

2 sprigs fresh cilantro, chopped

salt, to taste

1 Put all the filling ingredients into a food processor and blend to a medium paste. Chill for half an hour or so.

2 Put the all-purpose flour in a bowl and add some water gradually, mixing to form a stiff but pliable dough. Let rest for about 15–20 minutes, covered.

3 Roll the dough into 40 equal-size balls on a lightly floured surface. Individually, roll out each ball to a flat 2-inch circle. Put a generous tsp of filling in the center, and gather up the edges, crimping them together at the top, without leaving any flaps of dough, using a little water along the edges to help them stick.

4 Wash the chicken bones and put them into the bottom part of a steamer. Cover with water and bring to a boil.

5 Arrange the dumplings in a lightly oiled steamer basket — you'll need to do this in batches — and steam over the simmering stock and bones, covered, for about 12–15 minutes per batch.

6 Meanwhile, make the chutney. Char the tomatoes over an open flame or under a preheated hot broiler. When the skin is charred all over, remove it and discard. Chop the tomatoes in a food processor with the remaining ingredients.

7 Serve the dumplings warm with the chutney.

▣ Gyako
Chinese hotpot

In Calcutta we call this "chimney soup" because it cooks on the table in a charcoal cooker with a bowl around a chimney (known as a Mongolian hotpot). It is a Hakka dish, from the nomadic Chinese who settled in Calcutta. For 8 people you need 2 hotpots, with charcoal in the middle, which you can cook on the table. Or, you could use a deep stockpot with a lid and cook this on the stovetop.

Serves 8

9oz beef filet, thinly sliced

9oz pork tenderloin, cut into 2-inch strips

9oz boned chicken breast, skinned and cut into 2-inch strips

1 tbsp dark soy sauce

1½ tsp cornstarch

2 quarts strong clear bone stock, hot

1 small Chinese cabbage or bok choy

2 cups bean sprouts

1lb 2oz glass or rice noodles

Sauce 1

6 garlic cloves, peeled and finely chopped

3 medium fresh green chilis, finely chopped

½-inch piece fresh ginger, peeled and finely chopped

2 tbsp lemon juice

salt, to taste

Sauce 2

8–10 garlic cloves, peeled and finely chopped

1 tsp red chili powder

1 tbsp malt vinegar

1 tsp vegetable oil

½ tsp sugar

salt, to taste

Sauce 3

3 tbsp dark soy sauce

4–5 medium fresh green chilis, finely chopped

salt, to taste

1 Put the 3 meats in 3 separate dishes, and marinate each with 1 tsp dark soy sauce and ½ tsp cornstarch.

2 Meanwhile, make the sauces. Simply mix the ingredients for each in 3 separate bowls, adding salt if necessary.

3 If using the hotpots (*see* recipe introduction), fill the cooking bowls to just less than halfway with hot stock. Add half the meat to each bowl in layers, starting with the beef (which takes longest to cook), and finishing with the chicken. Add a layer of cabbage (or bok choy) and bean sprouts to each bowl, then arrange the uncooked noodles on top. Pour in as much stock as the bowls will take, and leave over the heat on the table to cook. Whoever is nearest can gently move the ingredients around, using their chopsticks. When the noodles are done and the meat is cooked through, the dish is ready to eat.

4 If using a stockpot, do exactly the same, but on a very low heat on the stovetop. Again, when the meat is cooked through and the noodles are soft, the dish is ready to serve.

5 The diners help themselves with their chopsticks and a ladle from the bowl in the hotpot. If you have a stockpot, transfer the ingredients to a serving bowl for each person and place on the table along with the sauce bowls.

পার্ক স্ট্রীট

PARK STREET

There's a passage in Vikram Seth's novel, *A Suitable Boy*, in which one of the characters, Lata, goes in a taxi to Park Street, only to find herself "taken aback by its unaccustomed brilliance." There was a time when Park Street was better known for its perpetual brilliance of lights, clubs, bars, restaurants, and other joints. But things change. Park Street still has a strong pull: it's still a flaming address to draw in curious moths, it still possesses the densest concentration of eateries and watering holes anywhere in the city, and the neon lights still shine brightly. And yet... and yet... it's not quite the same any more.

Park Street's life hasn't always been one of unalloyed glamour. After first being named Badamtala, it became Burial Ground Road (after what is now known as the South Park Street Cemetery), and then in the 1840s it was renamed after a deer park. There are even rumors that the mayor, Subrata Mukherjee, might throw everything up in the air and rename it once more, this time in memory of Mother Teresa.

The shape of the road on a map, with its clear diagonal line, infers a divide. It's therefore no coincidence that I was told by an old Raj hand that "an Englishman never lived north of Park Street." In flat geographical terms, the road links Park Circus and Lower Circular Road with Chowringhee. The traffic crawls up toward Chowringhee one way and then, in some sort of tidal-flow nightmare bang on the stroke of 2 P.M. it reverses direction and grinds slowly down thereafter. But, in mythical and behavioral terms, Park Street (and bits of the adjoining streets) has always been a place where the normal rules don't apply. The rest of Calcutta — indeed, the rest of India — has always lurked at its fringes, ready to criticize or condemn but unsure of precisely what is going on.

In a heyday that seems hazily elusive but is generally regarded to be somewhere after World War II up until the end of the 1960s, the Park Street area was crammed with food and entertainment. While establishments on Chowringhee such as the Grand Hotel and Firpo's were definitely black tie only, Park Street was far more bohemian. Maharajas mixed with dancing girls, there'd be 40 bands to choose from on any given night, a new Beatles tune would immediately be de rigueur in every musician's repertoire, and Indira Gandhi ordered shrimp cocktails from the Sky Room to be packed in ice and placed on the early evening flight to Delhi in order to get to her by dinner. Stories? Yes. But the aura of Park Street has long depended on such things. Many of the names of the musicians mean little away from Calcutta: Pam Crain, Anto Menezes, and Usha Uthup. Someone who registers a flicker is Biddu Appaya, who debuted at Trincas, and later produced hits such as Carl Douglas's "Kung Fu Fighting." Then, of course, there was the food with which Park Street became synonymous and which is still available in at least a handful of restaurants: "Continental cuisine." Which is what? Well, the best definition appears to be anything that is "distinctly not Indian, but produced with the ingredients that India has to offer."

To get to the high temple of "Continental cuisine" requires quick and nifty footwork. Past the Asiatic Society (at No. 1 Park Street, where it's been since 1804), past a cluster of evocatively named restaurants (the Ming Room, Blue Fox, Magnolia, Silver Grill, Kwality), past a gauntlet of beggar women with tiny babies in arms and street kids in a mix of rags and rip-off D&G T-shirts who tug equally at sleeves and consciences, past paan sellers with their shiny leaves, betel-nut, and other compounds, past Barista (India's infinitely superior answer to our standard coffee chains), past endless pavement magazine sellers and the Oxford Bookstore (By Appointment to: H.E. The Lord Mountbatten, and H.E. The Lord Irwin), past the lines for the *kathi* roll stalls and still on, past the new-look Flury's Tea Rooms. Left and around the corner leads very nicely to the front door.

Mocambo. A snap of the fingers, please! M-o-c-a-m-b-o. Now a restaurant, but when it opened in 1956, a nightclub serving food. Did the glitterati come for the chicken Tetrazzini or did they come to step onto Calcutta's very first glass dance floor with its colored lighting underneath? It's hard to tell. Either way, it became a huge success. A German interior decorator called Messerschmidt created an environment of such fabulousness that he was called on afterward to do up the Sky Room and the Blue Fox.

The first manager was an Italian, Mr. Prandi, and the first Indian chef was a Sikh poached from the Maharaja of Patiala. According to Mr. Kothari, the owner and son of the man who started it, "It was

always Continental or sometimes north Indian here — Bengali food was never the food of Park Street." His cooks have always been a mix of Bengali Christians, Mog cooks from Chittagong, and Muslims, producing a range of dishes that has altered little since 1956. And his waiters still wear their long jackets (or *chapkans*) with heavily embroidered turbans and cummerbunds. The menu cover is exactly the same, and its content suggests a style of cooking from another era:

> Deviled Pepper Crab:
> Whoooeee!
> There aren't enough Fire
> Alarms for these Babies!
> Order at your own risk!
> Rupees 120.00 (approx. $2.60)

Then there's mulligatawny soup, fish Florentine (using "beckty steak," of course), chicken Pavlograd (a version of chicken Kiev), surf & turf, and baked Alaska.

I lunch with food critic Nondon Bagchi, who explains the connection between this virtual time warp cuisine and the heavy influence of cooks who previously worked in the kitchens of British homes. "All sorts of mutations happened here: the invention of what we know as cutlets and chops, and things like Worcestershire sauce. The cook was thinking what to do to please his sahib's palette, but also about what will be interesting and new. Then, here in Mocambo, one day I ordered a Châteaubriand steak and it came with some boiled mixed vegetables that included a local item called snake gourd, which is long and waxy with soft-white flesh and seeds inside. Ingenious! It worked perfectly."

But there have been lean years on Park Street that have taken their toll. Nondon Bagchi recalls asking Mr. Ellis Joshua, the proprietor of Trincas, what was the most significant thing to change. The answer, he tells me, was one short sentence, "The Anglo-Indians went away." Many lived around this immediate postal code area in Calcutta 16 and they — along with large numbers of Goans — comprised many of the musicians, entertainers, waiters, cooks, and a large part of the audience as well. They went abroad in the tens of thousands in the 1960s.

There was much political and industrial unrest in the 1970s, with severe labor problems and the widespread introduction of trade unions. Power shortages were regular and hardly ideal if you operated an air-conditioned establishment. Much of the turbulence of that time meant capital flowed out of Calcutta and lent the city an air of neglect. Things stood still. Restaurants found themselves suspended in aspic.

But the pendulum swings of economic revival mean that, for every Mocambo, there's somewhere else where the new brooms of the 21st century are sweeping into every corner with a vengeance. Started by a Swiss owner, Flury's Tea Rooms became something of a fixed point on Park Street. "Flury's has always been the meeting place, the drawing room of the middle classes," I was told. In recent times, it's been under the ownership of the Paul family (whose Apeejay Surrendra Group owns the Park Hotel, as well as other freehold slabs of Park Street) and, frankly, they've gone for the blitzkrieg approach to makeovers — with a few dollops of fuchsia pink thrown in for a good measure. "Five generations of fine confection," it says outside. Not that you'd recognize much lineage from any of them once you cross the threshold. Now, it's all a whirlwind of froth, crushed nuts, kiwi slices, and frosting with cherries on top. Here, the chairs and banquettes have piping, just like the cakes.

Sitting in this puffed-up boudoir, I wonder where its reference points come from. There's nothing eastern Indian, or Bengali, or Raj-like, or even vaguely minimalist, about this new Flury's. No. This is a tearoom for the MTV generation, for people who'd truly prefer to be in some upscale enclave of Bombay. Diagonally across the street, I see what used to be the Modern Furnishing shop. Now, it's called The Tea Table. It has the same owners as Flury's and I discover it employs many of the old staff as well. Its cakes are laid out in the old display counters, and the room is furnished with the old chairs and tables. So, it's a sort of annex without the embellishments. I go across to see what it's like. An Anglo-Indian, Mr. Melvin Price is charm personified. The fans whirr, fresh-baked chicken patties waft out from the kitchen, and there's a tray of frosted chocolate cakes. This is a slice of recognizable Calcutta, but with a future that looks far from assured.

Roast bhetki Portuguese

Bhetki is highly prized by Bengalis for its flavor and lack of bones. This recipe uses filets, and almost all fishmongers in Calcutta will filet the fish for you. The "Portuguese" connection is in the use of peppers and tomatoes. Portuguese cooks were found in Park Street restaurants, and came from Portuguese settlements around Calcutta in places such as Bandel (famous for its many beautiful churches).

Serves 4

1 large piece *bhetki* (about 1lb 12oz), or cod or halibut filet

juice of 1 lemon

salt

½-inch piece fresh ginger, peeled and roughly chopped

4 garlic cloves, peeled and roughly chopped

1 tsp black peppercorns, crushed

2 tbsp vegetable oil

a few sprigs of fresh parsley, finely chopped

Sauce

4 tbsp butter

2 garlic cloves, peeled and sliced

1 medium red onion, peeled and finely chopped

¼ tsp turmeric

¼ tsp red chili powder

a pinch of sugar (or, more interesting, 2 tbsp port)

1 green sweet pepper, seeded and diced

1 red sweet pepper, seeded and diced

2–3 medium tomatoes, chopped

8oz can chopped tomatoes

1 Preheat the oven to 350°F.

2 Wash the filet of fish and pat dry. Use whole or, depending on the size of your oven and your dish, cut in half. Sprinkle with the lemon juice and salt to taste. Make a paste in the blender with the ginger, garlic, and black peppercorns, and rub this into the fish. Let marinate, covered, for about half an hour.

3 Meanwhile, make the sauce. Melt the butter in a small saucepan, add the garlic and onion, and cook for 2 minutes, until translucent. Add the turmeric, red chili powder, and sugar (or port), and fry for a minute. Add the green and red peppers and sauté for a minute. Add the fresh and canned tomatoes and stir. Cook on a medium heat for about 15–20 minutes, stirring occasionally, until thick. Taste for seasoning.

4 While this is cooking, heat the vegetable oil in a large ovenproof pan or casserole dish on the stovetop over medium heat. Brown the fish briefly on both sides, taking care not to break it while turning. Top the fish with the thickened sauce, and put the dish into the oven for about 15 minutes, covered. Turn up the heat to 375°F, and cook the fish for another 3–4 minutes, uncovered.

5 Serve immediately with some crusty Portuguese-type bread.

Deviled crab

Park Street reflected the cuisine of the West, and became a venue for the marriage of French-style cooking (with many French-influenced sauces such as béchamel, velouté, and espagnole) and Indian ingredients. This dish is inspired by two recipes from two different sources — the cook I learned from was more of a "devil" than Simon's, adding some chili and some garlic to the béchamel.

Serves 4

1 tbsp vegetable oil

1 onion, roughly sliced with its skin

4 garlic cloves, roughly sliced with their skin

6–8 black peppercorns

1 bay leaf

4 small or 2 medium crabs, washed thoroughly

1 tsp salt

about 1 cup grated Cheddar cheese

1 medium fresh green chili or ½ sweet green pepper, finely chopped (optional)

Mushroom béchamel sauce

6 tbsp butter

1 tbsp all-purpose flour

1¼ cups milk

salt

¼ tsp white pepper

4 medium cup mushrooms, sliced

paprika or red chili powder (optional)

½ tsp English mustard

⅛ cup dark rum

Garnish

2 medium eggs, hard-boiled and sliced

4 small sprigs fresh parsley

1 Heat the vegetable oil in a medium stockpot or deep saucepan over medium-low heat. Add the onion, garlic, peppercorns, and bay leaf, and fry until you get the aroma of cooked garlic. Add the whole crabs, turn around for a minute or so until they start turning red, then pour in enough water to cover them. Add 1 tsp salt. Once the water comes to a boil, remove any scum and simmer the crabs for about 12–15 minutes.

2 Remove the crabs and cool. Strain the stock, put it in another pan, and boil it for 3–4 minutes, again removing any scum if it forms. Set aside (we need a little for this recipe, save the rest to use as a fish stock).

3 Once the crabs have cooled, break off the claws, and pry away the bodies from the shells. Set the shells aside to wash and use later. From the body, discard the "dead mens' fingers" (the greyish finger-like gills). Crack open the body and extract the soft brown crabmeat. If there is any orange roe, add this to the meat. Crack the claws open with the flat side of a heavy knife and remove the white meat from the inside. Take care not to splinter the shells, as they can be very sharp. Flake the white meat and mix with the brown meat. Set aside.

4 For the sauce base, melt 4 tbsp of the butter in a small saucepan and then add the all-purpose flour. Stir or whisk until you can smell the flour cooking. Remove from heat and add just enough milk to form a stiff paste, stirring continuously. Add the remaining milk and mix well, then return to the heat. Bring it back slowly to a simmer and cook for 3–4 minutes. Add 2 tbsp of crab stock to make a sauce of coating consistency. Check the salt and add the white pepper. Set aside.

5 Preheat the broiler to medium.

6 In a shallow pan or a saucepan, melt the rest of the butter, then add the mushrooms. Cook for ½ minute, then add the paprika or red chili powder (if using), mustard, rum, and the crabmeat. Stir to mix well for 2–3 minutes, and then add the white sauce. Stir together well, then divide this mixture among the crab shells. Top with grated cheese and chili or sweet pepper if using. Broil for 1–2 minutes to melt the cheese and allow it to brown slightly.

7 Serve each topped with hard-boiled egg (you could make patterns with the whites and yolks) and a sprig of parsley.

Fish fry

Firpo's, now closed, was a well-known restaurant in Park Street for many years, and was responsible for elevating the simple fried fish of the domestic kitchen to restaurant status. This was done by cleverly using breadcrumbs. *Bhetki* is used in Calcutta, but you can substitute cod or haddock.

Serves 4

1lb 12oz flaky white fish filets (cod or haddock), cut into about 8 pieces

salt

juice of 1 lemon

2 medium eggs

1 tbsp all-purpose flour

1½ cups dried white breadcrumbs

vegetable oil

Marinade

1 small onion, peeled and finely chopped

3 garlic cloves, peeled and finely chopped

1-inch piece fresh ginger, peeled

3–4 black peppercorns, crushed

½ tsp turmeric

½ tsp ground cumin

½ tsp red chili powder

a pinch of sugar

¼ tsp garam masala (*see* page 21)

1 Put the fish in a suitable dish. Sprinkle with salt to taste and the lemon juice.

2 For the marinade, use a food processor to make a paste with the onion, garlic, ginger, and peppercorns, then mix with all the remaining marinade ingredients. Rub into the fish and let sit, chilled, for about half an hour.

3 Break the eggs into a bowl and mix thoroughly with the all-purpose flour. Put the breadcrumbs on a flat plate. Heat the vegetable oil in a deep-frying pan to medium-hot.

4 Dip each piece of fish into the egg-and-flour mixture, then coat well with breadcrumbs. Pat these in firmly.

5 Deep-fry the fish pieces in batches until crisp and golden, about 3–4 minutes. Drain well on absorbent paper towels.

6 Serve with tomato ketchup or *khashundi* (*see* page 190) and sliced onions.

Smoked fish

Park Street restaurants would traditionally use *hilsa* for this dish, and because the ambient temperatures in the city would not suit smoking as a style of safe cooking, they devised this technique to simulate the flavors of smoked fish. To get the most out of this recipe, use smoked salmon, but unsmoked white or oily fish would also be suitable. Start this dish at least a day before you want to serve it.

Serves 4

4 7oz pieces smoked fish

Marinade

juice of 1 lemon

¼ tsp fresh ground white pepper

salt

about 4–5 small anchovy filets

1 tbsp olive oil

1 tbsp *khashundi* (mustard sauce, *see* page 190)

Sauce

4 tbsp butter

1 white onion, peeled and finely chopped

5 tbsp *khashundi*

2 tbsp light cream

1 Using a mortar and pestle, blend the marinade ingredients to a fine paste. Marinate the fish pieces in this paste, covered, in the refrigerator overnight (or even for a couple of days if you like).

2 Make the sauce first. Melt the butter in a small saucepan, add the onion and cook until translucent. Add the *khashundi* and simmer for a minute, then remove from the heat. Mix in the cream. Set aside to serve separately, at room temperature.

3 When ready to eat, preheat the broiler to medium.

4 Broil the fish pieces for 10–12 minutes, turning once. The fish is traditionally served with the sauce and sautéed vegetables.

Chicken Tetrazzini

This is a club and restaurant dish of Calcutta, and could have been created by or for an Italian, but the word "Tetrazzini" now refers to the fact that noodles or spaghetti are used in the dish. You can roast the chicken as below, or buy an already roasted chicken.

Serves 4

2–3 tbsp vegetable oil

2lb 4oz–2lb 12oz fresh chicken

salt

2 carrots, roughly chopped

1 onion, peeled and roughly chopped

1 celery stalk, roughly chopped

1 bay leaf

6–8 black peppercorns

Tetrazzini

4 tbsp butter

4 garlic cloves, peeled and sliced

2 medium onions, peeled and finely sliced

1 green sweet pepper, seeded and sliced

6–8 medium button mushrooms, sliced

1¼oz dried spaghetti, cooked

salt

fresh ground white pepper

1 tbsp dark rum (or, better I think, 2 tbsp white wine)

béchamel sauce as on page 128 using only butter, flour, and milk

1 tsp English mustard

3 tbsp grated cheddar cheese

finely chopped parsley

1 Preheat the oven to 350°F.

2 Put a roasting tray on top of the stove and heat the vegetable oil over medium-low heat. Brown the chicken on all sides, then remove from the tray and sprinkle with salt to taste. Add the vegetables, bay leaf, and peppercorns and place the chicken on top. Roast in the oven for 20 minutes, then baste, cover with foil, and roast for another 1½ hours. Remove the foil, and check for doneness (if the juices run clear when the flesh is pierced, the chicken is ready). Return the chicken to the oven for 5 or so minutes as required to crisp the skin a little. Remove the chicken from the tray and cool.

3 Skin the chicken, and remove the meat from the bones. Cut the meat into medium strips.

4 Preheat the broiler to medium.

5 To make the rest of the dish, melt the butter in a pan, add the garlic and onion and cook for 3–4 minutes, or until the onion is lightly brown. Add the pepper and mushrooms and sauté for a couple of minutes. Add the roast chicken strips, cooked spaghetti, salt and pepper to taste, and the rum (or wine). Boil to reduce the liquid, then add in the béchamel sauce and mustard. Stir well over a gentle heat, to bring the sauce up to a hot temperature.

6 Pour into a baking dish and top with the grated cheese. Broil until golden brown, about 5–6 minutes. Serve hot, sprinkled with some parsley.

Chingri cutlet

"Cutlet" is usually a cut of meat, but here the term is applied to a large freshwater shrimp — *chingri* — that is butterflied, spiced, dredged in crumbs, and fried. Only restaurants in and around Park Street could afford to buy these large shrimp, and afford the time involved in preparing them. As a result, the Bengali housewife has been happy to leave this dish to the professionals.

Serves 4

4 colossal shrimp, weighing about 7oz each, or 8 jumbo shrimp, about 3½oz each

1 cup toasted dried breadcrumbs (*see* tip below)

vegetable oil

1 lemon, cut into wedges

Marinade

1 small onion, peeled and roughly chopped

3 garlic cloves, peeled and roughly chopped

½-inch piece fresh ginger, peeled and roughly chopped

2 medium fresh green chilis, roughly chopped

½ tsp garam masala (*see* page 21)

2–3 black peppercorns

½ tsp turmeric

2 tsp Worcestershire sauce

a pinch of sugar

1 Shell the shrimp and remove the heads (keep these for another dish). Leave the tails on. Devein the shrimp: slice all the way down the back, but not through, then open them out and wash out the black intestine. Open the shrimp out further by slicing into each side of the flesh and unfolding them outward to make large ovals or pear shapes with the tail at one end. Put the shrimp in a dish.

2 In a food processor, blend the onion, garlic, ginger, and chilis together to a fine paste, then mix in the remaining marinade ingredients. Rub this paste on all sides of the butterflied shrimp and let marinate for about half an hour.

3 Put the breadcrumbs on a flat plate. Heat the vegetable oil in a frying pan over medium heat. Dip the shrimp into the breadcrumbs and press down to coat well on both sides.

4 You have to fry the shrimp individually at first. Put one shrimp in the oil, and hold it down with a flat spoon to prevent it from curling. Cook for about 1½ minutes, then turn and cook for another 1½ minutes. Once the shrimp has been turned, it will not curl up, so you can add the next one. Proceed in this way until all the shrimp are cooked.

5 Drain on absorbent paper towel, and serve with a wedge of lemon and some *khashundi* (*see* page 190) or tomato ketchup.

tip: Restaurants use bread crumbs to get rid of excess bread. Households would use fresh soft crumbly bread, but for this dish the dried toasted crumbs are more suitable. Toast the bread, or bake it, until golden, then reduce it to crumbs with a rolling pin (or in the blender).

Sago, coconut, and jaggery pudding

This is also called "three-palm pudding," because it is made from sago (a light starch obtained from the stem of various palms), coconut, and new-season date-palm jaggery. It would be made by chefs rather than at home, and appears on the menu of several Park Street Continental-style restaurants. It is a typical winter dessert, as you get fresh date jaggery only in the months of January and February.

Serves 4

½ **cup large-grain sago**

1 fresh coconut

about 1 cup water

⅜ **cup liquid date-palm jaggery (***jhola gur* — **use a good maple syrup if no jaggery can be found, but the taste won't be exact)**

1 Soak the sago in cold water, enough to cover, for about half an hour (the grains will swell to about 2 inches in diameter). Drain and put into a pan of enough boiling water to amply cover the sago. Boil for about 3 minutes, or until it turns translucent — which is the starch cooking. Drain and reserve the sago in cold water to cover.

2 For the coconut milk and cream, break open the coconut, retaining the water from inside (*see* tip on page 159). Grate the flesh. Squeeze the flesh in fine cheesecloth to extract the thick milk (from 1 coconut, you should get about ½ cup thick milk). Set this aside. Put the squeezed flesh in a bowl, add about 1 cup warm water, and soak for 2–3 minutes. Strain through the cheesecloth again into a bowl, then squeeze again to get some thin milk. Add the coconut water to this thin milk and mix in the drained sago.

3 Traditionally, 3 bowls are placed on the table, in which you have the sago, the thick coconut milk, and the liquid jaggery. You take a spoonful of each and mix them together in your own individual bowl. But you can mix all 3 together, taking care not to make it too runny (pour off a little of the thin coconut milk from the sago), and serve all as one pudding.

Almond soufflé

The soufflé, introduced during the Raj, was a trademark of and the pride of clubs and restaurants catering for the elite of Calcutta. It was an alternative to the syrupy Bengali sweets, and is one of the few Bengali desserts to contain eggs. Because gelatin is also used, many orthodox Indians were, and are, reluctant to indulge. Soufflés can be tricky to make, so be careful with each step and use your intuition.

Serves 4

4 large eggs

⅔ cup superfine sugar

1 tbsp lemon juice

2 tsp powdered gelatin

½ cup sliced almonds

1½ cups heavy cream

2 tbsp ground almonds

½ tsp almond extract

1 Separate the egg yolks and reserve the whites. Put the yolks in the top of a double boiler. Add half the sugar to the yolks and mix well to dissolve the sugar. Add the lemon juice. Heat gently, whisking all the time. Once the water starts steaming, cook for about 3–4 minutes.

2 Meanwhile, dissolve the gelatin in as little water as possible. Add to the yolk mixture in a steady trickle, whisking continuously. Remove the pan from the heat and pour the mixture into a bowl. Put in the fridge to set for an hour. It will still be a thickish liquid at this point.

3 Lightly toast the sliced almonds and then let cool.

4 Whip the cream to soft peaks and fold into the yolk mixture, along with the ground almonds and almond extract. Whip the egg whites with the remaining sugar to firm peaks, and fold that in as well.

5 Rinse a 2-quart soufflé dish with water and allow excess to drip away (this eases the unmolding). Line the bottom with the toasted almond slices, and gently spoon in the fluffed mix. Chill for 3–4 hours, or longer if you wish.

6 To serve, unmold onto a platter.

জলখাবার ও রাস্তার খাবার

SNACKS AND
STREET FOOD

Calcutta's epicenter has got a tongue-twister of a title: Binoy-Badal-Dinesh Bagh, named after three young freedom fighters from the 1930s who met sticky ends after shooting the inspector general of prisons. Trams clanking in that direction merely say BBD Bagh. Before that, it was Dalhousie Square and before that Tank Square, Great Tank, and Lal Dighi. Unsurprisingly, a massive square tank of water still sits in the middle of what was once the commercial and administrative heart of India. There are still Writers' Buildings on the north side and the General Post Office on the west (with its plaque marking the site of the "Black Hole of Calcutta" tucked into an arch). But much of this history and landscape today is obscured by the dazzle and rush of pavement life. It's an opera played out over and over again, almost but never exactly the same: the minutiae of human activity under awnings and beside makeshift stoves, against a backdrop of thundering traffic with its taxi-horn highs and fume-belching lows and its choir of polished white Ambassador government cars claiming to be "on duty."

I watch a stall-holder make egg-toast, which he sells for 5 rupees (10¢) a portion. His stove is fired by kerosene. He brought his eggs in from the country, where he stays. There's a shallow omelet pan of about 7 inches in diameter into which he pours nut oil and lets it smoke. In goes a beaten egg, some salt, chopped onion, green chili, chopped cilantro leaves, and — like some sort of soundtrack over which he has no control — he keeps shouting "eggtoastfiverupees," but it merely gets lost in the din. In goes a slice of white bread that looks partly toasted already. He presses it into the egg, then turns it over and presses again. He tips it onto a wooden block, cuts it in half, quarters it, throws on pepper and coarse-grained salt. And that's it. Delicious. Like a masala omelet with a bread filling. He might sell a hundred or so egg toasts in a day. This single microproduction line is repeated in and around all these streets thousands upon thousands of times each working day. And if it isn't egg-toast, then it's biryani, *rumali roti* (paper-thin handkerchief breads) served with *achar* (pickle), *shingara* (Bengali snack samosas), *moghlai porotha* (crispy bread stuffed with ground meat and fried), chow mein, chili chicken, sweets, and of course, chai.

Near the intersection with Hare Street, behind the civil courts, street vendors share space with rows of typists, men who sit on the pavement with their typewriters cranking out a form of *babu* English ("I beg to bring to your kind attention...") or typing up affidavits. Some copy draft letters for their customers from books, such as *100 Most Common Complaint Letters*. Next door, under polyethylene awnings, lunch is underway. The man who runs this stall has his umbrella hooked up on the back wall and a little auspicious symbol of limes and chilis strung up together. His menu offerings are relatively sophisticated — *shukto*, fish fry, bitter gourd, and a curry made with papaya and *posto* (poppy seed). He even employs a man to make sweets such as *sandesh*. There's a mighty stove glowing with hot coals that stays lit until 9 P.M.; then the fires are put out but he and the men he employs sleep here. He begins again the next day at 6 A.M. and tells me "*Unoon e aanch dite hoye*" ("I have to light and stoke the fire to cook the food"). He starts stoking the fires first thing and sends a boy out to get the fish as the streets are being swept. And the whole thing rolls around all over again.

This is the way vast swathes of Calcutta take their food — certainly the midday meal for the hundreds of thousands, probably millions, who form part of clerical Calcutta, filling in giant dusty ledgers in government offices in the business district. The surroundings might not be plush or calm, the air quality might not be the purest, but the range of food on offer is both staggering and affordable. A man visiting on business from Santiniketan always eats in this vicinity. "The quality is good. It doesn't affect the health or the stomach," he tells me reassuringly. And oddly, despite the communal washing of clothes taking place no more than a few yards away, I think I know what he means. "In Santiniketan, price is higher and taste less good. This mutton biryani is very fresh and must be consumed straightaway."

I shift to the marginally quieter S.N. Banerjee Road in the poorer and largely non-Bengali area of Dharamtala, which is full of what are known as *paise* hotels (or *hotul* as it's pronounced here). Don't let the title fool you: these are little more than the stalls on the street but in pukka buildings with proper roofs. The name comes from "*paise*," the smallest coin in

Indian currency before conversion to the metric system. The Mahamaya is one such. It seats 12 people on benches and, during the day, fish is cooked in mustard oil with rice and, in the evenings, no rice, only *rotis* (breads). This is a hangover from the rationing days of World War II, when rice and wheat were limited. So, rice at lunch, *roti* at night. And they make their *rotis* on the pavement just to show how fresh they are.

Farther along, at the base of a dilapidated palace built by the benefactress Rani Rashmoni, I meet a young *chattoo-wallah* in his late teens, I'd say, who makes a thick protein drink the consistency of emulsion paint by mixing *chattoo* or ground chickpea flour (which is complete with a drawing of a body-builder on the packet) with salt, lime juice, onion, green chili, chili powder, and water using a large wooden swizzle stick. For 2 rupees, a large glassful gives energy and cools the stomach. "If you pull a rickshaw all day," he tells me, "with this you won't be hungry until the afternoon." I ask where he's from. "Bihar, after Muzaffarpur," he replies, "where the best lychees come from."

:: Aloo keema chop
Potato and lamb croquettes

Snacking is an integral part of Calcuttan culture. A busy day for the average working man would be interspersed by tea breaks fortified with savory snacks in which the tea stalls specialize. The snacking would be accompanied by animated discussions ranging from politics and soccer to fine art and music. And if the snacks were appreciated enough, some would be taken home to be shared by loved ones.

Makes 12 croquettes

5 medium potatoes, boiled, peeled, and mashed

salt

2 medium fresh green chilis, chopped

½ tsp cumin seeds, toasted and finely ground

2 sprigs fresh cilantro, finely chopped

2 medium eggs

2 cups fresh white bread crumbs

vegetable oil

Filling

1 tbsp vegetable oil

1 medium onion, peeled and finely chopped

14–18oz lean ground lamb

½-inch piece fresh ginger, peeled and chopped

½ tsp red chili powder

½ tsp ground coriander

¼ tsp ground cumin

½ tsp garam masala (*see* page 21)

juice of ½ lemon

salt

1 Put the mashed potatoes in a bowl and add salt to taste, the chilis, cumin, and cilantro, and mix well.

2 For the filling, heat the 1 tbsp vegetable oil in a pan, add the onion, and cook until light brown, about 3–4 minutes. Add the ground lamb and all the other filling ingredients except for the garam masala and lemon juice. Stirring continuously, cook for about 18–20 minutes, until the lamb is cooked through. Add the garam masala, lemon juice, and some salt to taste. Put the mixture in a sieve and allow any excess oil to drip out and the mixture to cool.

3 Divide the mashed potato into 12 equal portions, and form each into a ball. Put the ball in the palm of your hand, and make a depression in it with your forefinger. Put 1 tbsp of the ground lamb filling into this depression, and fold the potato over and around it. Flatten with your hands to form a round patty. Do this with all 12, and chill, covered, for 15–20 minutes.

4 Beat the eggs in a bowl and put the bread crumbs on a flat plate. Heat the oil for deep-frying in a *karai* or heavy wok to a medium hot temperature. Dip each patty into the egg, then coat with some bread crumbs. Deep-fry until golden brown, about 5–6 minutes. Drain on absorbent paper towels and serve hot. These croquettes are traditionally served with fresh sliced onions and carrot and beet salad.

:: Kathi kabab roll
Spiced meat and bread kebabs

This might have been Calcutta's first experience of fast food. This kebab, rolled in an egg-coated bread, was made famous by a restaurateur called Nizam-Uddin, and hence the dish is also known as "Nizami roll." Usually beef would be used, since it was a Muslim-style dish, but lean lamb can be substituted.

Makes 8 rolls

1lb 2oz filet of beef, cut into strips about 2 inches by ½ inch

salt

vegetable oil

Marinade

2 medium onions, peeled and roughly chopped

1-inch piece fresh ginger, peeled and roughly chopped

4 garlic cloves, peeled and roughly chopped

2-inch cinnamon stick

4 green cardamom pods

1 black cardamom pod

8–10 black peppercorns

1 tsp Szechuan pepper

1 tsp cumin seeds

1 tsp turmeric

salt

2 tbsp vegetable oil

Bread

4¼ cups all-purpose flour

⅓ cup plus 1 tbsp fine semolina

about 1 cup warm water

1 tbsp vegetable oil

3 medium eggs

½ tsp turmeric

2–3 sprigs fresh cilantro

Salad

2 medium onions, peeled and sliced into rounds

2 medium tomatoes, halved and sliced

1 medium fresh green chili, sliced

juice of 1 lemon

1 For the marinade, grind the onion, ginger and garlic to a paste. Toast all the spices except for the turmeric to crisp them, about 1½ minutes, then grind to a fine powder. Mix these with the turmeric, salt to taste, and the 2 tbsp vegetable oil. Rub into the meat strips, and let marinate in the fridge, covered, for 3 hours or overnight.

2 To make the bread, sift the all-purpose flour into a bowl, them mix in the semolina and some salt to taste. Make a well in the center, and gradually add enough warm water, up to 1 cup, to form a soft pliable dough. Rest the dough for 3–4 minutes, then add the vegetable oil. Knead the oil in to make the dough more pliable. Divide this into 8 balls, cover with a moist cloth and let rest for 5 minutes.

3 For the bread, break the eggs into a mixing bowl, and whisk lightly with a pinch of salt, the turmeric, and cilantro.

4 Heat some vegetable oil in a shallow frying or omelet pan, preferably nonstick, over medium heat for pan-frying.

5 Roll out the dough into rounds as thin as possible. If you let the rounds rest after a first rolling the gluten will relax, and then you can roll the rounds even thinner.

6 Spoon a layer of beaten egg on top of the rolled bread circles, one at a time. Slip them, again one at a time, into the pan, egg-side down, then spoon another layer of egg on top. Once the egg cooks on the lower side, flip the circle over and cook the other side, no more than 3 minutes in all. Drain on absorbent paper towel and keep warm. Do the same with the other 7 circles.

7 Preheat a broiler or a barbecue (in the latter case, you will have to skewer the meat first). The heat should be very high to sear the meat rapidly on all sides. Cook the meat in batches. The total cooking time should be about 3–4 minutes.

8 For the accompanying salad, simply mix all the ingredients together.

9 Divide the meat into 8 equal portions and place across the middle of each bread circle. Put some of the fresh salad on top, and roll the bread around the filling. In Calcutta, this is then rolled in paper, to be eaten in hand as you walk. This is a more convenient way of eating for busy people.

:: Shingara
Fried pastry triangles with savory filling

One of the most popular anytime street snacks Bengalis enjoy, this recipe is also known as samosa in other parts of India. Bengalis are a bit more adventurous with their fillings, so you could come across quite a variety of *shingaras*. The tea stalls make hundreds of them every day, so it's easier to buy them than to make them at home.

Makes 16

4 cups all-purpose flour

½ tsp black onion seeds

2 pinches of salt

1 tsp vegetable oil

about ¼ cup warm water

Filling

vegetable oil

3 medium potatoes, peeled and cut into ½-inch cubes

1 small cauliflower, broken into small florets

about 15 unsalted peanuts, without shell and skin, halved

2 tsp ground coriander

½ tsp ground cumin

½ tsp red chili powder

salt

a pinch of sugar

¼ tsp garam masala (*see* page 21)

2–3 sprigs fresh cilantro, chopped

1 To make the dough, sift the all-purpose flour into a bowl (this sifting is very important). Mix in the onion seeds, salt, and 1 tsp vegetable oil. Make a well in the center, and start to add the warm water, a little a time, mixing until you have a firm, pliable dough. You might not need all the water. Let the dough rest for about 15 minutes, then divide it into 8 balls. Let them rise, covered with a moist cloth, while you prepare the filling.

2 For the filling, heat vegetable oil for deep-frying to medium-hot in a large *karai* or heavy wok, and fry the cubed potatoes for about 6–8 minutes, until soft. Remove and drain. Increase the temperature of the oil slightly and fry the cauliflower florets for 2–3 minutes to color them slightly. Remove and drain. Put the oil pan to one side.

3 Heat 1 tbsp of the frying oil in another *karai* or heavy wok, and add the potato, cauliflower, and all the remaining filling ingredients. Use a wooden spoon to make this mixture into a coarse filling, breaking up the cauliflower and potato. Cook for 5–6 minutes to allow the spices to release their aromas. Set aside to cool.

4 To make the casing, roll each dough ball (using flour for dusting, or oil, as you prefer), into a large circle about ⅒-inch thick. Cut in half to form 2 half-moons. Moisten the edges of the half-moons with water and make a cone shape. Fill each cone with the filling, not quite to the top, but dividing it equally. Bring the 2 sides of the rim together and press to seal. If you want to make the perfect *shingara*, press this sealed side down on a work surface to form a base on which the triangle can sit.

5 Heat the *karai* containing the vegetable oil for deep-frying to less than medium-hot. Fry in batches for about 20 minutes: the shell has to cook very gradually until it is crisp and light golden brown.

6 Eat hot with sweet, milky tea.

Chicken kobiraji cutlet
Egg-fried marinated chicken

A traditional Bengali family would see this as a treat when they were out, as chicken is not commonly cooked in Bengali households. Chicken breasts are marinated in spices, then dipped into beaten or whisked eggs, and pan-fried to a frilly and lacy finish. The Parsees make a similar dish and call it "lacy cutless."

Serves 4

1 chicken, about 1lb 12oz in weight

vegetable oil

2 medium eggs

¼ tsp turmeric

3 sprigs fresh cilantro, chopped

a pinch of salt

1 tbsp warm water

1 tbsp all-purpose flour, diluted with 2 tbsp water

Marinade

½-inch piece fresh ginger, peeled and roughly chopped

2–3 medium fresh green chilis (depending on the heat you like), chopped

1 tsp turmeric

6–8 black peppercorns, crushed

1 tsp garam masala (*see* page 21)

1 tsp ground cumin

½ tsp red chili powder

salt

1 Skin the chicken and remove the meat from the bone, leaving the breasts and legs whole. You will use 4 pieces, the 2 legs and the 2 breasts (save the rest for making stock). To make the dish look appealing, the wing bone and the knuckle joint of the leg can be left attached to the meat. Beat the chicken pieces lightly with a meat hammer to flatten and tenderize.

2 In a mortar and pestle, grind the ginger and green chilis to a paste, and then mix with all the remaining marinade ingredients, including salt to taste. Put the chicken pieces in the marinade, turning, and then let sit for at least half an hour.

3 Heat the vegetable oil in a frying pan to medium-hot.

4 Beat the eggs until frothy. Add the turmeric, cilantro, salt, and warm water (*see* tip), and beat again. Coat the chicken with the flour paste, and dip each piece of chicken into the egg mixture. Pop the chicken into the oil, laying it out flat very gently. Turn a couple of times while frying and, when golden, after about 7–8 minutes, ladle 1 tbsp of the egg mixture over the top of the chicken. As soon as this fluffs up, remove the chicken to absorbent paper towel to drain.

5 Serve hot with tomato ketchup.

tip: The warm water is important, as it slows down the cooking of the egg, allowing the egg to froth up.

:: Ghugni
Curried chickpeas

This is one of the most popular and nutritious street foods to be found in every corner of Calcutta. It is also something that every household would make at least once a week as a daytime snack. Some people include cubes of mutton (never lamb in India — always mutton), usually for special occasions.

Serves 8

3 cups dried chickpeas (or two 15oz cans cooked chickpeas)

1 large bay leaf

5 green cardamom pods

3 cloves

1-inch cinnamon stick

1 tsp cumin seeds

1 tsp coriander seeds

½ cup ghee

2 medium potatoes, peeled and cubed

½ fresh coconut flesh (*see* page 159), finely sliced

1 large onion, peeled and finely chopped

1 tsp red chili powder

½ tsp fennel seeds, crushed

2 tsp turmeric

salt

Garnish

2 tbsp thick tamarind pulp

1 tbsp hot water

2 tsp grated jaggery

a pinch of salt

¼ tsp ground cumin

¼ tsp red chili powder

1-inch piece fresh ginger, peeled and cut into very fine strips

2 medium fresh green chilis, cut lengthwise into quarters

2–3 sprigs fresh cilantro, chopped

1 If using the dried chickpeas, soak them overnight in enough water to cover. Drain, cover with fresh water in a large saucepan, bring to a boil, and boil for 10 minutes before reducing the heat and cooking for another 50 minutes at a steady simmer. Watch the level of the water. Drain the chickpeas, then cover again with cold water. Rub gently with your fingers to loosen the skins, which will float to the top. Discard the skins and drain the chickpeas. If using canned chickpeas, simply rinse, drain, add fresh water, and rub off the skins as above.

2 Toast the herbs and spices for a minute or two, then grind to a fine powder in a mortar and pestle.

3 Heat the ghee in a *karai* or heavy wok to medium-hot, and first fry the potato cubes to a light golden brown, making sure they are cooked through. Remove and drain on an absorbent paper towel. In the same pan, fry the coconut slices until light brown, then drain. Add the onion to the pan, and fry until just turning light brown. Add the red chili powder, crushed fennel seeds, turmeric and chickpeas with some salt to taste (the canned peas are pre-salted, so go carefully). Return the potatoes to the pan and add enough water to come halfway up the chickpeas. Cook for 2–3 minutes, until the mixture heats through, then add the ground roast spice mixture and mix this in well.

4 To serve, mix the tamarind and water with the jaggery, salt, cumin, and red chili powder. When the jaggery has melted, drizzle this on top of the chickpeas. On top of that add the ginger, chilis, and cilantro.

Moghlai porotha
Aromatic flaky bread

The Moghlai *porotha* is similar to any other *paratha* from any other part of India, but the way we spell it is based on the way the Bengalis roll their "o"s and "r"s while referring to this delicious bread. This is a perfect accompaniment for the Muslim *paya* and chicken *dopiaza* on pages 94 and 99.

Makes about 8 porothas

4 cups all-purpose flour, plus extra for dusting

¼ cup plus 2 tbsp fine semolina

½ tsp sugar

a pinch of salt

about 5 tbsp ghee

a few saffron strands

4 tbsp milk

about ½ cup warm water

vegetable oil

1 To make the bread dough, sift the all-purpose flour into a bowl. Mix in the semolina, sugar, and salt. Rub in 2 tbsp of the ghee to get a coarse breadcrumb consistency. Add the saffron to the milk. Make a well in the crumbly flour and pour in the saffron milk. Steadily knead into a firm dough, adding the warm water as you progress. It is advisable to let the dough sit for only a couple of minutes between water additions — you don't want the gluten to start expanding at this stage. Cover with a moist cloth and let the dough rest for 20 minutes.

2 Divide the dough into 8 equal portions, roll into balls, and let sit again for 5 minutes, covered. Roll out as thin as you can, using flour for dusting: you want eight 8-inch circles.

3 Spread a fine layer of the remaining ghee onto each circle and dust it with flour. Roll the circle to form a rope shape, and spiral the rope to form a tight circular bun. Rest, covered, for 20 minutes. Using your palms, flatten each bun, then roll it out to about 2-inches thick. You will see the layers.

4 Moisten a suitable frying pan with a little vegetable oil and heat to medium. Add 1 *porotha* at a time and cook, turning over a few times, until crisp, golden, and cooked through. Serve hot.

:: Coolotolar raan kabab
Barbecued lamb kebab

Coolotola is the name of a predominantly Muslim area of Calcutta, and this dish is found at street-side eateries, which open up early in the evening to cater to office workers on their way home. It's a cheap way of eating protein. Because this dish takes so long to cook at home, people order it in advance: they often line up at the stall before it is open, then leave their own containers with the cook to be filled.

Serves about 8
3 lamb shanks, 4lb 8oz in all

Marinade
1 tbsp white poppy seeds
4 1-inch cinnamon sticks
2 black cardamom pods
6 green cardamom pods
4 cloves
2 tbsp fennel seeds
1 tbsp cumin seeds
1 tsp Szechuan pepper
2 onions, peeled and chopped
8 garlic cloves, peeled and chopped
1-inch piece fresh ginger, peeled and roughly chopped
3–4 fresh green chilis, chopped
6–8 fresh mint leaves
2 tsp turmeric
1 tsp red chili powder
2 tbsp vegetable oil
salt

Sauce
1-inch piece fresh ginger, peeled and roughly chopped
6 garlic cloves, peeled and chopped
2 tbsp vegetable oil
2 bay leaves
3 onions, peeled and finely chopped
1½ cups plain yogurt
1 tsp turmeric
2 tsp chickpea flour
2 tsp red chili powder
2 tbsp ground coriander
1 tsp ground cumin
a few saffron strands
salt
a few drops of rose water

1 Either buy meat trimmed of all fat and sinews by the butcher or do it yourself. With a boning knife or a skewer, make deep, even holes in the meat all over.

2 To start the marinade, toast all the spices and then grind to a fine powder. Blend the onion, garlic, ginger, chilis, and mint to a fine paste, and mix with the turmeric, red chili powder, vegetable oil, salt to taste, and the ground toasted spices. Rub this marinade well into the meat, and let sit for about an hour, or longer.

3 Preheat the oven to 375°F.

4 Put the lamb on a baking tray in the oven and cook for about 20 minutes.

5 Meanwhile, for the sauce, use a mortar and pestle to blend the ginger and garlic together to a paste. Heat the oil for the sauce in a deep ovenproof pan. Add the bay leaves and onion, and allow it to turn light brown, then add the ginger-garlic paste. Mix the yogurt in a separate dish with all the remaining sauce ingredients except the rose water. Take the onion pan off the heat and add the spiced yogurt. Mix well, then return to the heat, and gently simmer for 2–3 minutes. Add 1½–2 cups water and bring back to a simmer.

6 At this point, the lamb should have finished its 20 minutes cooking. Remove it from the oven, and place it in the deep pan with the sauce and its cooking juices. Remove any excess fat. Add salt to taste and the rose water. Cover the pan and return it to the oven, with the temperature reduced to 350°F. Cook for about 2 hours, occasionally ladling the sauce over the lamb.

7 Remove the lid, baste, and return to the oven for another 15–20 minutes, or until the meat is very soft and tender.

8 Serve with loads of crunchy sliced onions and sprigs of mint. It's eaten in the street: you'd get a bowl, holding soft meat and sauce, with bread baked in a wood-fired oven to dip.

বাঙালী মিষ্টি

BENGALI SWEETS

There is a wonderful phrase used in certain Calcutta establishments: "We have no branch shop." It's stamped across the boxes of the confectioners and sweet makers, Girish Chandra Dey & Nakur Chandra Nandy, and reads like a point of honor, plain and simple. It positions a retailer at the opposite end of the mercantile spectrum from, say, a Wal-Mart. You'll only find our goods sold by us from this single establishment and nowhere else, is what it's really saying.

Girish Chandra Dey & Nakur Chandra Nandy is on the small Ramdulal Sircar Street opposite a ladies' college in a rabbit warren of narrow lanes in the heart of north Calcutta. It's existed since 1844 (or 1251 if you use the Bengali calendar), and is singular in the production of the very thing that can make most Bengalis either go wild with excitement or melt into floods of nostalgic tears (especially if they're far from home): *sandesh*. The word means "news," and it's a sweet made from sweetened fresh milk curds (or *chhana*). That's it, basically, although the whole thing is reminiscent of a paint chip showing only endless shades of white and beige; *sandesh* has infinite degrees of subtlety depending on factors such as the type of sweetening agent, the time of year, the shape, and the use of additional ingredients and flavorings. Some Bengalis are happy to try new variants, but for Bengali purists (which is how most see themselves), the *sandesh* is immutable and they know exactly what's what.

Behind the green-painted metal grill of the shop-front lies a small series of rooms and a cramped little courtyard where everything takes place: milk pasteurization, manufacture, and packaging; staff feeding and washing — and it's a communal dormitory. People drift in and out and cardboard boxes cascade willy-nilly underneath framed photographs of garlanded gods. At first glance, it's not possible to realize quite how industrious the men who work here are and how seamlessly they work. But then, usually in the late afternoon/early evening, the milk arrives and the slackness of the middle of the day evaporates. Milk churns arrive from nearby Jorasanko milk bazaar with — to my amazement —

straw packed in the top to prevent spillage. After straining, the raw milk gets pasteurized in a big, black iron *karai*, heated from underneath by what sounds like a blast furnace but, in fact, uses only kerosene. It's stirred using what almost looks like an archaeological implement called a *jhanti*, a great wooden stick cut from the stem of a date tree.

Next up, the milk is curdled by the addition of whey gathered from previous sessions. This is done in great cotton-lined bowls which, once the milk has separated, are gathered up and left to drain so the whey water is collected in earthenware pitchers, ready to be used again. Another man, squatting low on the ground and with the build and demeanor of a meditating wrestler, takes over, weighs the *chhana* and then starts to rub it into a much finer texture. This stage is critical to the quality of the *sandesh*. His technique can strongly determine the characteristics and reputation of the entire operation. One of the shop's owners leans across and says, "To what extent you rub and massage the *chhana* now is secret. It's a kind of feeling you cannot measure — that's the beauty of it."

The *chhana* returns to another *karai* to be cooked with sugar or jaggery and, if it's winter, with *gur* (new-season date-palm juice). Again, they're very hush-hush about the proportions involved. Far more visible is the finishing process. Another group of men sitting in another corner take some cooked, cooled *sandesh* mixture and put it in small individual molds, make imprints using their thumbs, pour in spoonfuls of liquid *gur*, a few ground pistachio nuts, and then close the gap with a gobstopper-size bit of *sandesh*. They then tip them out and move on to the next batch. Mr. Prasanta Nandy tells me that this sweet originates in the town of Chandernagore, and that it was traditionally meant to be given to sons-in-law. They'd bite into it, spill the liquid *gur* everywhere, causing them much embarrassment and their parents-in-law even more amusement.

In Bengali, confectioners have always been referred to as *moiras*. I ask Mr. Nandy if he's the *moira*, or is it one of the team engaged in a pivotal activity. He cackles without restraint... "Here, everyone is *moira*," he replies, continuing, "you don't go to the cricket club in London and ask who is the cricketer, do you?" Indeed, I learn later that the *moiras* are a confectioner caste in Bengal. They are definitely close-knit — one has worked here for 30 years, another for 15 years and his father was also here for almost 60 years. All are from villages in either west Bengal or neighboring Bihar, and many are from around Chandernagore, north of Calcutta, which was an old French enclave. In trying to find out the history of Bengali sweets, someone mentioned that certain *sandesh* owed something to the French éclair, in technique if not in taste or ingredients.

According to Dr. K.T. Achaya in his book *Indian Food: A Historical Companion*, Bengalis appear to have possessed sweet tooths since time immemorial. There's always been an ample supply of fresh milk needing to be used up quickly and there's no hard-cheesemaking tradition. These two factors have meant the development of a vast range of sweets based on milk and milk solids (*khoa*). Apart from the *sandesh*, there's an enormous list of items: some in syrup, some not; some using curdled milk, others using thickened or even condensed milk (*kheer*); and a separate league incorporating rice (sometimes powdered, sometimes whole) and semolina. Then there are the flavorings: saffron, rose water, orange zest, pistachio, and cardamom. Some, generically called

pithas, are made in the home especially for when visitors come to call. There's *pitha payesh*, *puli-pitha*, and *chitoi pitha* to name but three of the infinite ways of interpreting rice-, wheat-, and coconut-based dishes.

But much of this domestic tradition is waning as extended family networks shrink. In many ways, Bengalis and sweets are akin to the French and pâtisseries. Why spend ages making it when there's a perfectly decent professional who can (invariably) do it better at the end of the street? And Calcutta is awash with sweet shops. There are chains such as Ganguram's; there are specialists such as K.C. Das (where the famous *rosogolla* was invented); and there's also the once-rarefied outlet of Bhim Chandra Nag, much of whose reputation rests on the fact that it was called upon by Lady Canning, the then Vicereine of India, to come up with a new sweet. What is known today as the *ledikenni* is still being trundled out alongside other variants such as chocolate *sandesh* and apple *sandesh*. Relying as they do on poor-quality flavorings, this school of sweet-making is best glossed over.

At the other end of the spectrum, there are north Calcutta confectioners who are so understated and discreet that they make things merely for a few chosen long-established families. One such producer makes a *sandesh* called *satpakebandha*, which has seven layers, each one with a different color and flavor. You may be served one, but it's highly unlikely you'll ever be taken by your hosts to the shop.

What shines through visiting places such as Girish Chandra Dey & Nakur Chandra Nandy is that using Bengal's rich supplies of milk in the myriad ways that it does is as old as its history. Historically, while milk was always boiled to keep it from spoiling, there have been cloudy issues around whether it was right to sour milk (upper-caste Hindus claimed that once you put something into milk to curdle it, that milk was rotten, and therefore had to be discarded). But what is clear is that, in all the years of the Raj — the odd *ledikenni* notwithstanding — the British never sought to take much of an interest in Bengali sweet-making. Perhaps it was too far of a leap, and here was an industry that could never have been of any direct or immediate benefit to them.

Narkoler naaru
Coconut dumplings

Quite a few Bengali sweets use coconut. I don't recommend using desiccated; fresh coconuts are widely available (and while you're at it, buy a coconut grater or scraper, too — they're not very expensive). These dumplings should be eaten at room temperature, at any time of the day. They are used as a bribe for children: "If you drink your glass of milk, you can have a *naaru!*"

Makes 12 dumplings

1 quart whole milk

3 cups fresh grated coconut (*see* **tip**)

¼ cup sugar or date jaggery

1 Bring the milk to a boil in a large pan, then reduce the heat and simmer for about 40 minutes to reduce, stirring continuously. Keep scraping the milk from the sides. You want to end up with about 1 cup thick milk.

2 Add the coconut and sugar to the milk, and transfer to a *karai* or heavy wok. Cook over a very low heat, stirring continuously, until the whole mass is quite dry. This could take another 40 minutes. The mixture, when it is ready, will have come together into a ball.

3 Remove the thick mixture to a bowl or flat work surface and, when cool enough to handle, form into 12 balls. You might need to grease your palms lightly with some vegetable oil. Set aside to cool.

tip: To extract the flesh from a whole coconut, hold the coconut firmly and hit it on a hard surface, very sharply and smartly. This should crack open the shell. Alternatively, hold the coconut in your hand and hit it with a hammer. Try to do both operations over or near a bowl in order to catch the water, which is sweet to drink. Then use a coconut scraper or grater to remove the sweet white flesh from the inner casing.

❖ Payesh
Bengali rice pudding

Bengalis like their desserts very sweet, so you should add sugar to taste. If you don't like your rice pudding too sweet, feel free to reduce the quantity of sugar, but not the jaggery, as this will add taste along with sweetness. *Payesh* is wonderful eaten chilled the next day, and it is usually served with *luchis*, but it can also be served warm.

Serves 4

1 cup basmati rice

1 quart whole milk

⅓ cup sugar, or to taste

1 tbsp grated jaggery (date jaggery is preferable if available)

⅛ cup raisins

seeds from 4 green cardamom pods, crushed

1 Wash the rice and soak in enough water to cover for 20–30 minutes, then drain.

2 Add the rice to the milk in a thick-bottomed saucepan, and simmer over medium heat until the milk is reduced by almost half. Stir occasionally so that neither the rice nor the milk sticks to the bottom.

3 Add the sugar, jaggery, raisins, and cardamom, and simmer for another 5 minutes, still stirring. When the rice is very soft and the sugar and jaggery have melted, bring it to a quick boil to thicken it.

4 Serve hot or cold.

 ## Pantua
Sweet semolina and cottage cheese dumplings

The filling is usually made with whole milk that has been boiled down until it is dry; the natural cream then allows it to be fried to the consistency of a thick paste. This substance is readily available in Bengal, but in its absence we can use powdered milk.

Makes 20 dumplings
1 recipe cottage cheese (see page 145)
1¼ cups fine semolina
½ cup all-purpose flour
2 tsp ghee
vegetable oil
1 tbsp sugar

Thick syrup
2¼ cups sugar
1 cup water

Thin syrup
⅓ cup plus 1 tbsp sugar
seeds 2 green cardamom pods, crushed
2 cups water

Filling
1 tbsp raisins, soaked and drained
2 tbsp powdered milk

1 To make the thick syrup, dissolve the sugar in the water and cook gently until the syrup reaches 230°F, thread stage (put your fingers in iced water, dip your forefinger and thumb quickly in the syrup, and the syrup should form a fine thread between them). Set aside. To make the thin syrup, dissolve the sugar with the crushed seeds in the water and cook gently, 10–15 minutes.

2 Make a stiff dough with the cottage cheese, semolina, all-purpose flour, and 1 tsp ghee. Form this into 20 equal-size balls. Mix the ingredients for the filling with 1 tsp ghee, then cook for a few minutes over a gentle heat. Let cool a little. Heat some vegetable oil to medium-hot, or until a tiny piece of the dough rises slowly to the surface when dropped in.

3 Meanwhile, make an indentation in each dough ball and insert ½ tsp of the filling. Mold the dumpling back into a round shape, covering the filling. Dust the balls with the sugar.

4 Deep-fry the balls until dark gold in color. Transfer as cooked to the thin syrup and soak for 10 minutes. Dip into the thick syrup and serve warm or cold.

Ledikenni

Semolina and cottage cheese dumplings

This is named after Lady Canning, Lord Canning's wife, and is a sweet she was known to relish. The only difference between this and the *pantua* above is that *ledikenni* is not soaked in the thick syrup. After frying, it is soaked in the thin syrup (which removes the frying oil), then it is dusted with superfine sugar and served as is. It is a much drier sweet and much less syrupy.

Aam kheer
Milk and ripe mango pudding

Toward the end of the mango season, when the fruits start getting overripe and people are tired of eating them as a fruit, they are cooked with milk to make a delightful dessert. Try to use fleshy mangoes as opposed to the stringy varieties. This pudding can be eaten at any time of the day as it is not too sweet.

Serves 10–12

1½ quarts whole milk

¼ cup sugar

1 tbsp rice flour

3 medium ripe sweet mangoes, peeled and cut into cubes

½ tsp green cardamom seeds, crushed

1 Heat the milk in a heavy-bottomed saucepan. Add the sugar and heat gently until it all dissolves, stirring occasionally. Increase the heat a little and gently reduce the milk to half its volume, about an hour, stirring as often as you can and scraping the milk from the sides of the pan.

2 Once reduced, add the rice flour and stir to mix in. Add the mango cubes and simmer for 5 minutes. Sprinkle in the cardamom seeds.

3 Pour into 10–12 individual small bowls and chill. The mixture will set to a soft jelly.

❧ Puli pitha/dudh puli
Tiny coconut dumplings in sweetened milk

This dessert is a must during the monsoons. It marks the birth of Lord Khrishna, usually around mid-August in Bengal. The dish is laborious, so it is not made at any other time of year. The technique is passed down, usually from mother to daughter-in-law. If you can't get date jaggery, just use sugar instead (plus about an extra ⅓ cup).

Serves 4

½ fresh coconut, grated (*see* page 159)

⅔ cup sugar

2 cups all-purpose flour

about 1 cup water

3½ cups whole milk

⅔ cup grated date jaggery

seeds of 2–3 green cardamom pods, ground to a powder

1 Cook the coconut and sugar in a *karai* or heavy wok over low heat until the sugar melts and mixes uniformly with the coconut — about 12–15 minutes. Remove from the *karai* and cool. It will thicken.

2 Mix the all-purpose flour with the water, and cook this very slowly in a *karai* until the water evaporates and the flour comes together in a lump. Mash it with a wooden spoon.

3 You now need to make tiny balls of this mixture, about ¼-inch in diameter. Take a small pinch of the mixture at a time, and roll it between your forefinger and thumb to form a ball. Do this with all the dough, preferably while it is still warm (which is why you need some other hands to help you). When all the balls are made, flatten them individually into discs of about 1-inch in diameter. Put a little of the coconut mix into the middle, close it, and roll into a torpedo shape, fat in the middle and tapered at the ends.

4 If you are still awake by the end of this, heat the milk in a large shallow pan, bring it to a boil, stirring continuously, and simmer to reduce to about 3 cups. Scrape the sides of the pan as the milk reduces. To this add all the dumplings, and the milk will thicken to become like a pudding. Add in the date jaggery, and cook for 4–5 minutes, gently swirling the pan around until the jaggery dissolves.

5 Serve cold, sprinkled with ground cardamom seeds.

◈ Bhapa doi
Steamed sweetened yogurt

This creamy, sliceable, textured pudding is similar to a crème caramel — one of my favorites. The sweetness of the condensed milk works wonderfully with the acidity of the plain yogurt.

Serves 4

3⅛ cups natural yogurt

1 cup sweetened condensed milk

seeds of 6 green cardamom pods, powdered in a mortar and pestle

8–10 saffron strands

Garnish

sliced pistachio nuts

1 Heat some water in a steamer. If you do not have a steamer, set a small, metal flat-bottomed bowl upside down inside a larger pot with a tight-fitting lid. Fill the larger pot with water and bring to a simmer. Put the item to be steamed into a suitable dish, cover with plastic wrap, and place atop the upside-down bowl to steam.

2 Mix the yogurt and other ingredients in a cool glass bowl and aerate it rapidly with a hand whisk. Do not whip too much for fear of the whey separating. Pour it into 4 individual serving bowls, cover with plastic wrap and put in the steamer or on top of the upside-down bowl. Cover with a lid and steam on a steady simmer for 35–40 minutes.

3 Carefully remove the bowls and then let cool. Remove the plastic wrap and chill.

4 Serve chilled, sprinkled with the sliced pistachio nuts.

Rosh bora
Light lentil dumplings in syrup

This hot and sweet dish is enjoyed during the monsoons — a time when a family is at home, unable to go out, and there is more time to cook and appreciate more complicated dishes. *Rosh bora* would be eaten as a midday or early evening snack, rather than as a dessert after a meal.

Serves 4

1 ¼ cups yellow split lentils

½ cup fine semolina

2 tbsp plain yogurt

vegetable oil

1 tsp ground fennel

a pinch of salt

Syrup

1 cup grated date jaggery (or cane jaggery)

¼ cup plus 1 tbsp sugar

3 ½ cups water

a few saffron strands

1 Soak the lentils in enough water just to cover for about an hour. Add the semolina and blend to a very smooth and thick paste. Add the yogurt, mix it in well, and let sit in a warm place for a few hours (or overnight if made in the evening).

2 To make the syrup, dissolve the jaggery and sugar in the water. Bring to a boil, skim, then gently simmer for about 20 minutes. This will make a fairly thin syrup. Add the saffron and keep warm.

3 Heat the vegetable oil to medium-hot. Add the fennel and salt to the slightly aerated lentil mixture (a result of the yogurt souring a little), and gently fold it in. Oil a tablespoon, and take ½ tbsp of the lentil mixture at a time. Drop it into the oil and fry in batches until dark gold in color and puffed up, about 8–10 minutes.

4 Each dumpling has to be drained very well, then dunked in the warm syrup while the fritters are still hot. Remove from the syrup and eat warm.

❧ Ranga aloor rasher pitha
Juicy sweet potato pancakes

This dessert is made during the spring months of the year from February to April, which is when you can get hold of excellent date-palm molasses and jaggery. If you can't find these, use normal jaggery (made from sugar cane) flavored with a dash of honey.

Makes 12 pancakes

6 medium sweet potatoes, washed

3 tbsp all-purpose flour

1 tbsp rice flour

2 tbsp vegetable oil, plus extra for deep-frying

Filling

1¼ cups fresh grated coconut (see page 159)

1 cup whole milk

4 tbsp grated date-palm jaggery

Syrup

1 cup date-palm molasses or jaggery

2 cups water

1 Boil the sweet potatoes whole until soft, about 30 minutes, then peel and mash them. Mix the flours together and rub in the 2 tbsp oil until the mixture is like crumbs. Mix this thoroughly into the mashed sweet potato, and let rest for about half an hour. After this time, form into 12 equal-size balls.

2 For the filling, cook the ingredients together in a *karai* or heavy wok over low heat until the jaggery melts. Reduce until the mixture becomes quite dry, but still pliable. Let cool, then form into 12 equal-size balls.

3 For the syrup, mix the molasses or jaggery with the water and simmer until reduced by about a quarter, about 20 minutes. Let cool a little, until syrup is warm but not hot.

4 Take a ball of the sweet potato dough and make an indentation in the middle. Fill this with a ball of the filling. Bring the sides over to cover the filling, then roll out into a flat disc with about a 2-inch thickness.

5 Heat the vegetable oil for deep-frying to medium-hot, and deep-fry the pancake discs until golden brown, about 5–6 minutes. Remove, drain, and then dunk them into the syrup. These are served cold.

❧ Gokul pitha
Coconut dumplings

This is another coconut dumpling made to celebrate Lord Krishna's birthday in and around mid-August. It is also quite elaborate in technique, so works well when there are two or three people involved in the preparation.

Makes 25 dumplings
1¼ cups all-purpose flour
a pinch of baking powder
about 1 cup water
ghee

Syrup
1¼ cups sugar
2¼ cups water

Filling
2 quarts whole milk
2½ cups fresh grated coconut (*see* page 159)
¼ cup sugar

1 Make the syrup first. Simmer the sugar and 2¼ cups water together to melt the sugar, then boil until thread stage (*see* page 161). The syrup should be thick.

2 For the filling, reduce the milk to 2 cups over medium-low heat. This will take about an hour. Keep scraping the sides of the pan. Add the coconut and sugar, and keep reducing until it forms a firm, tight mixture. Cool and divide into 25 equal-size balls.

3 For the batter, beat together the all-purpose flour, baking powder, and water until smooth.

4 Heat the ghee to a high heat.

5 Dip each filling ball into the batter and deep-fry in batches in the hot ghee for about 4–5 minutes, until golden. Remove using a slotted spoon and drain on absorbent paper towels.

6 Put the fried dumplings in the syrup and let cool. Serve chilled.

আচারবিচার এবং উৎসব অনুষ্ঠান

RITUALS AND
CELEBRATIONS

As the stifling heat of summer and the sapping humidity of the monsoons start to fade in the final weeks of September, strange things happen. Teams of men tug long carts piled high with bamboo poles to every neighborhood. These are speedily assembled into buildings and, within days, these structures are transformed into makeshift temples or *pandals*. They might have domes or minarets or pay homage to the Eiffel Tower, but their raison d'être is to house an image of Calcutta's most revered Hindu goddess, Durga, as well as her children and the demon she slays. For four days in October, good triumphs over evil as the city's most prized festival, *Durga Puja*, envelops virtually the entire population in a spectacle of light, music, prayers, sightseeing ("visit our top five *puja pandals*" trumpets *The Calcutta Telegraph*), shopping (Benarasi silk saris 50 percent off for *Puja*), and food.

Today, the *pandal* is the center of attention and public manifestation of each community, or *para*. Monies are raised and each *para* sets up a way of feeding its people with food each day (known as *bhog*). But this is a modern interpretation, as in years gone by *Durga Puja* was a more private affair that took place in large family houses and palaces. I once witnessed a *puja* in the faded magnificence of the Laha House in north Calcutta. A makeshift roof, complete with ornate chandelier, filled in what would have been the courtyard to allow all 120 family members to carry out their ceremonies. Rows of lamps, their wicks dipped in ghee, were lit; the sound of drumming echoed around the high walls; and the stage (*thakurdalan*) with Durga at its center was decorated with banana plants, fruits, rice, coconuts — *prasad* or food offerings to the gods. Vast meals were cooked: *khichuri* some days, always *luchis*, huge amounts of *aloo dum*, *dal* and *kheer* (a reduced, evaporated milk). The food would be vegetarian on certain days and utterly non-vegetarian on others. And everywhere there would be endless amounts of sweets, especially *sandesh*; trays shared around, boxes brought by well-wishers and relatives, and boxes packed up ready to take on to other gatherings.

There's a popular saying in Bengal that there are "13 feasts in 12 months," but it's always seemed to me that 13 is way off target. Auspicious days crop up with remarkable regularity. Someone told me that his grandmother must have observed at least 30 festivals. In addition to *Durga Puja*, there are *pujas* held for *Kali*, *Lakshmi*, and *Saraswati*. I watched Professor Tapan Raychaudhuri, in his sitting room in North Oxford, as his eyes glazed over recalling the festival of *Nabanno*. This is celebrated, particularly in rural areas, when the rice has been harvested and a mixture of raw rice and young coconut is served with milk and jaggery. "It's paradisiacal, although, to be frank, I haven't eaten it in the last 50 years," he says. And leading up to the great Muslim festival of *Id-ul-Zoha*, to mark the end of Ramadan, goats are taken through Calcutta's streets in order to be slaughtered, particularly around the Chitpur Road near the Nakhoda Masjid, toward Park Circus and Metiabruz.

Other rituals have a softer edge. *Jaimangalbar* is performed solely by women and takes place in the fierce summer during the mango season. It involves a meal of a creamy mix of yogurt, sweetened milk, mangoes, and bananas to appease the gods. And then there are the ritual floor paintings using rice flour, known as *alpana*, again carried out by women, this time to mark *Laxmipuja*.

From birth to death, food is an integral marker, a rite of passage, ebbing and flowing and giving rhythm to the seasons and years. Before a baby is born, a pregnant woman undergoes a *sadh* ceremony, where women eat a simple meal of fish. When a child is six to eight months old, there's the *annaprasan*, or the first rice ceremony, after which rice and other foods replace a mother's milk. For Brahmins, there's the sacred thread ceremony where, for three days, a boy eats only vegetarian items, after which a tremendous family feast usually ensues.

And then there are weddings — a vast industry in Calcutta in their own right, and what's being served at a wedding can determine attendance. Where's the reception being held? Is Bijoli Grill doing the catering? Or is it Munnar Maharaj? I've yet to attend a reception where alcohol is served (one I went to didn't even go so far as to provide soft drinks), and I turned up somewhere else where the menu trumpeted Kantaki Fried Chicken. A quick twist of the vowels and the sad truth become clear — although this tasted far better and far, far spicier than the dish after which

it was named. Unfortunately, so far as Hindu weddings are concerned, gastronomic delicacies are rare. The middle classes seem to be in awe of a buffet with fish — *rui* if you're lucky, biryani, mutton curry, and, if my track record is anything to go by, always ice cream.

One of the only two *shrad* ceremonies I've been to was for R.P. Gupta in 2000. It took place, as tradition dictates, on the 11th day after his death. All the tables and chairs and garlanded photographs were arranged in the specially cleared parking garage underneath the building he had lived in, in Mandeville Gardens, the very same one I'd first journeyed to years before. All his friends and family were there. What did we eat? I have absolutely no detailed recollection, other than that this was the most delicious series of vegetarian items I have ever eaten. I'm sure there were greens and cauliflower dishes, stuffed *patols* and other gourds, plenty of *luchis* and preparations involving *channa*. Out of simplicity came great richness and out of death came a divine feast.

Chorchori
Mixed vegetable stew

Chorchori is a typical dish served as one of the courses at a wedding feast. It adds balance to the meal. Bengalis tend to overcook their vegetables, but if you leave them crisp you will not get the same enjoyment: the finish of a well-cooked *chorchori* should be silky. A *chorchori* would be transformed into a *chanchra* by the addition of fish heads or unshelled shrimp, and this, too, is a typical wedding dish.

Serves 4

2 medium potatoes, peeled and cubed

2 medium eggplants, peeled and cubed

2 cups peeled pumpkin flesh, cubed

1 cup young fava beans in pod (or sugar snap peas)

2 tbsp vegetable oil

1 tsp panch phoran (*see* page 54)

1 large onion, peeled and sliced

1½ tsp turmeric

1½ tsp red chili powder

a pinch of sugar

salt

4 medium fresh green chilis, cut lengthwise in halves

1 Wash the potato, eggplant, pumpkin, and beans together, drain and put into a *karai* or heavy wok with about 1 tbsp water. On a low heat, cover and cook until the vegetables start to soften, about 5 minutes.

2 In a separate large pan or *karai* or heavy wok, heat the vegetable oil, and fry the panch phoran until it crackles. Add the onion and fry until soft, about 5 minutes. Add the turmeric, red chili powder, sugar, and salt to taste, and transfer the vegetables to this. Mix well. Cook, adding about 2 tbsp water, until the pumpkin and eggplant are very soft and the potatoes are cooked through, about 20–25 minutes.

3 Check for seasoning, increase the heat, and dry off any excess liquid. Add the green chilis and serve hot with boiled rice. (The hotter you want it, the earlier you add the green chilis.)

NOTE: If you want to add the fish heads or unshelled shrimp, cut them up into small pieces and fry them in mustard oil. Add them to the dish when you add the mixed vegetables and spices.

☐ Bangla polao
Spiced rice with cashew nuts and raisins

Bangla polao is the integral hub of a wedding feast. Spicy curries and fries are complemented by this aromatic, slightly sweet rice. The dish is often presented strewn with rose petals (in winter) or jasmine petals (in summer), depending on the season. Crisp and brown fried onions would be an edible alternative to petals.

Serves about 12

12 cups basmati rice

1½ cups shelled cashew nuts

⅓ cup raisins

⅞ cup ghee, plus 1 tbsp

1-inch cinnamon sticks

6 green cardamom pods

4 cloves

2 small dried bay leaves

¼ nutmeg, grated

½ tsp powdered mace

¼ cup sugar

2 tsp rose water

salt

2 tbsp whole milk

a big pinch of saffron strands

Garnish

rose or jasmine petals, or crisp fried onions (*see* page 61)

1 Wash and soak the rice for about 20–30 minutes. Drain. Soak the cashew nuts and raisins separately in water to cover, to soften them, about 15 minutes. Drain.

2 Heat the ⅞ cup ghee in a deep ovenproof pot with a lid on the stovetop over medium-low, and add the cinnamon, cardamom, cloves, and bay leaves. Allow them to brown slightly, then add the drained rice. Fry for 2–3 minutes, stirring carefully (you don't want to break the grains), then add enough hot water to cover the rice by about 1½ inches. Cover and simmer until almost half the water is absorbed, then add the nuts, raisins, nutmeg, mace, sugar, rose water, and salt to taste. Cover again, and simmer until most of the water has been absorbed, about 15–18 minutes.

3 Preheat the oven to 350°F.

4 Meanwhile, in a small saucepan over low heat, warm the milk with the saffron and drop the remaining 1 tbsp of ghee in it. When the water has been absorbed by the rice, stir the rice once, gently, then level the top and pour the saffron milk over the whole dish. Cover and put into the oven for about 20 minutes. After this time the rice will have completely absorbed the water and the grains will be cooked through.

5 Remove from the oven, loosen the rice with a flat spoon, and transfer to a warmed serving dish. Serve garnished with the aromatic flower petals or crisp fried onions.

tip: The soaked cashew nuts fluff up when they are added to the dish toward the end, and have a wonderful soft, creamy texture. Cashew nuts added to hot oil at the beginning of a dish would be much firmer and not nearly so interesting.

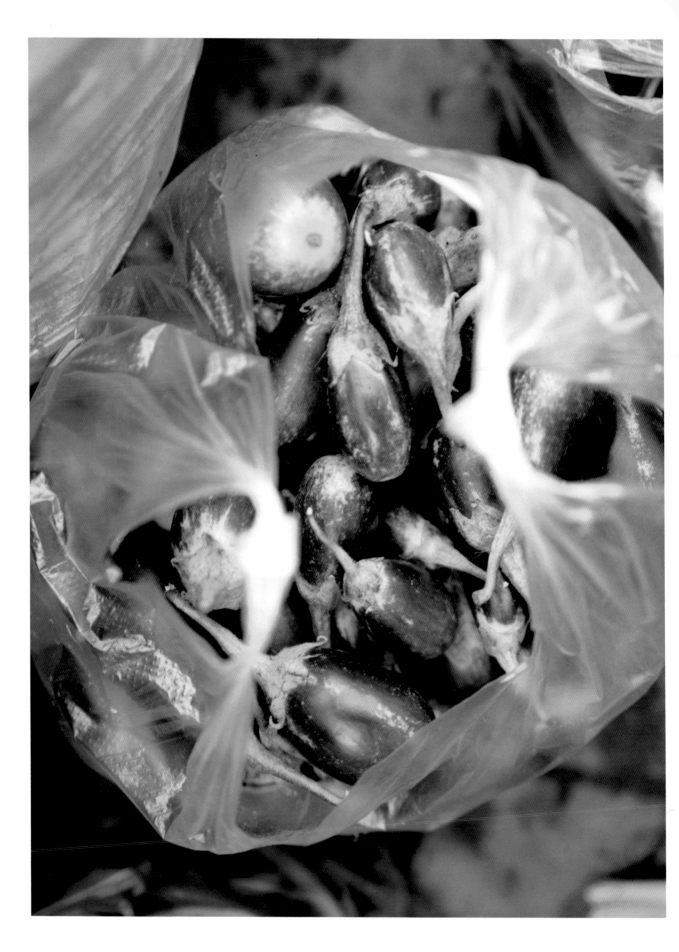

Paanch shobji bhaja
Spiced fried vegetables

The combination of five vegetables is used as a religious offering in the worship of the goddess of wealth, Laxmi. The dish usually includes potatoes, pumpkin, wax gourd, beans, and okra, but you could also use eggplants and other similar vegetables. The gourd used here is what we call *patol*: it is like a plump gherkin, rugby-ball shaped with dark and light green stripes.

Serves about 12

about 12 wax (or ivy) gourds

3 medium potatoes, peeled and cut into thin rounds

2 cups chopped fresh okra

1lb 2oz red pumpkin, peeled, seeded, and cut into rectangles of 1¼ inches by ½ inch

4 cups runner beans, trimmed and stringed, cut into 1¼-inch pieces

3 tsp turmeric

1 tsp red chili powder

2 tsp ground cumin

a pinch of sugar

salt

2-inch piece fresh ginger, peeled and ground to a paste

2 tbsp all-purpose flour

about 2 tbsp water

vegetable oil

1 To prepare the gourds, cut the ends off and scrape off the waxy outer skin with the back of a knife. Cut them in half. A pale whitish color of flesh would indicate a tender, ideal vegetable; if it is reddish it's overripe and not suitable. Prepare all the other vegetables, and keep in separate containers. (It may be best that they are kept apart, but from this point they are treated in the same way.)

2 Mix the powdered spices with the sugar and salt to taste. Divide into 5 portions. Coat each vegetable with a portion of the mixed spices. Mix the ginger equally between the vegetables, then dust them with the all-purpose flour. Sprinkle with water to make the flour stick.

3 Heat the vegetable oil in a *karai* or heavy wok, and individually fry the vegetables in batches. The potatoes and pumpkin will take about 5 minutes; the okra about 3–4 minutes; and the gourd and beans about 2 minutes.

4 This is best enjoyed with *khichuri* (*see* page 62) or dal (*see* page 60), and boiled rice.

◻ Peper chutney
Green papaya chutney

Green papaya chutney is a welcome change to tomato chutney on wedding menus in spring (March and April are the wedding months). Its translucent, light-green color is very attractive. It is not an accompaniment, as most chutneys would be, but a course in its own right. It is served after the hot curries, to prepare the palate for the sweets to follow, with poppadoms. In India we would use a mango-flavored ginger — *aam ada*.

Serves about 12

2 medium green papayas

a walnut-sized piece of seedless tamarind

1½ cups water

1-inch piece fresh ginger, peeled and roughly chopped

1 small green mango, peeled, stoned, and roughly chopped

2 tbsp mustard oil

¼ tsp mustard seeds

½ cup raisins

6 medium dried red chilis, seeded and torn into pieces

about ¼ cup sugar

salt

1 tbsp all-purpose flour

1 Peel the papayas and remove the seeds. Cut into 1-inch-wide slices, about 2 inches thick. Boil the papaya in hot water until just turning soft, about 10 minutes, then drain.

2 Soak the tamarind in the water for about 15 minutes, then rub through a sieve to extract the thick pulp plus liquid. Blend the ginger and mango together to a paste.

3 Heat the mustard oil in a pan to smoking hot. Cool slightly, then add the mustard seeds and allow them to crackle. Add the raisins and dried chilis. When the raisins balloon, add the boiled papaya and the sugar. Stir-fry for a couple of minutes, then add the tamarind pulp, its liquid, and salt to taste. Add enough water to just cover the mixture, then simmer for 8–10 minutes, allowing the papaya slices to start disintegrating.

4 Dissolve the all-purpose flour in a little water to make a smooth thick paste, and add this to the chutney. Simmer for another 3–4 minutes, allowing the flour to cook out, stirring continuously to avoid lumps forming or the mixture sticking to the bottom.

5 Just before removing from the heat, stir in the ginger-mango paste. Serve at room temperature, ideally with fried poppadoms.

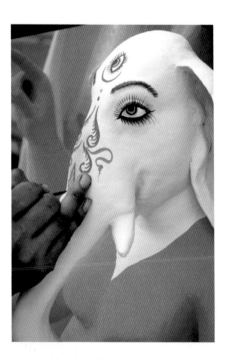

Dokar dalna
Lentil cakes in gravy

Dhokar dalna forms the protein content of a vegetarian meal, and it is cooked when feeding Brahmins after a funeral. It is such a wonderful dish that it is now enjoyed as part of any meal, by both vegetarians and non-vegetarians alike.

Serves 4

1½ cups yellow split peas

½ fresh coconut (*see* page 159)

½-inch piece fresh ginger, peeled and made into a paste

2 tsp turmeric

1 tsp red chili powder

2 medium fresh green chilis, finely chopped

salt

3 tbsp ghee

½ crisp fried onions recipe (*see* page 61)

vegetable oil

Gravy

1 tbsp vegetable oil

½ tsp cumin seeds

2–3 small dried bay leaves

1-inch piece fresh ginger, peeled and chopped

2 tsp turmeric

1 tsp red chili powder

1 tbsp ground coriander

1 tsp ground cumin

1 cup plain yogurt

⅞ cup coconut milk

1 tsp garam masala (*see* page 21)

salt

a pinch of sugar

about 1 cup water

3 potatoes, peeled and cut in quarters lengthwise

1 tbsp ghee

1 Wash the yellow split peas and soak in water overnight. The next day, drain and grind to as smooth a paste as possible.

2 Grate the coconut and mix the ground split peas, coconut, ginger, turmeric, red chili powder, and fresh chilis with salt to taste. Add the ghee to this mixture, and cook it in a *karai* or heavy wok over medium heat for about 15–20 minutes, stirring continuously. When the mixture is thoroughly heated through, it will start leaving the sides of the *karai*.

3 Chop the crisp fried onions, then add them to the dal mixture. Mix in well, and transfer to a round, flat metal plate with sides (a *thala*), or a shallow pie dish. Press down evenly and, using an oiled knife, cut into diagonal criss-cross shapes, about 1 inch across, so they look like diamonds. Let cool.

4 Meanwhile, make the gravy. Heat the 1 tbsp vegetable oil in a *karai*, add the cumin seeds and bay leaves, and allow to crackle. Add the ginger and the ground spices, and fry for a minute. Add the yogurt, coconut milk, garam masala, some salt to taste, and the sugar. Simmer for a couple of minutes, then add about 1 cup water. Simmer until a pouring consistency is achieved, about 3–5 minutes.

5 Heat enough vegetable oil for deep-frying to medium-hot in a *karai* or heavy wok, and fry the potato wedges until light brown in color. Drain well and add to the still-simmering gravy. Simmer until the potatoes are cooked through, which should take about another 4–5 minutes. Remove the gravy and potatoes to a serving dish.

6 Now, in the same deep-frying oil, fry the diamonds of dal mixture until golden brown and crisp, about 3 minutes. Drain well on absorbent paper towel and arrange in the gravy in a single layer. Swirl around, top with the ghee, and serve immediately; otherwise the cakes will lose their crispness and the gravy will dry up. Serve with boiled rice.

☐ Malpoa / janamastami
Pancakes flavored with fennel in syrup

Malpoas are made to celebrate Lord Khrishna's birthday in mid-August, on the eighth day of the celebration. They are crisp on the edges and very soft in the center, oozing syrup, and are often topped with the cream skimmed off the top of boiled milk.

Makes 8–10 pancakes

1 quart whole (not homogenized) milk

1⅔ cups all-purpose flour

1 tsp fennel seeds, crushed

To cook and serve

ghee

1 thin syrup recipe (*see* page 161), with a few saffron strands in it, warmed

1 tbsp shelled pistachio nuts, chopped

1 Boil the milk to reduce it to about 1 cup, stirring and scraping the sides continuously. Let cool. Skim off the cream which sets on top and keep it for later.

2 Sift the all-purpose flour into a bowl, make a well in the center, and little by little mix in enough of the reduced milk to form a smooth paste. Add to this the fennel and the rest of the milk to form a batter. Add some water, up to ½ cup: what you want is a medium-thick batter which would coat the back of a spoon.

3 Heat the ghee to medium-hot in a nonstick 8–10-inch frying pan. Using an ⅛ cup ladle, spoon some batter into the ghee. Gently swirl the pan so that the batter spreads out. Allow the pancake to cook for 2–3 minutes on one side, then flip it over and cook for another 2–3 minutes. Drain well, then plunge into the warm, saffron-flavored syrup. Serve with the reserved cream and pistachio nuts.

4 Do the same with the rest of the batter to make the remaining pancakes.

Nonta puli
Sweet potato and green pea cakes

Nonta puli consist of rice flour and sweet potato mash, filled with lightly spiced green peas. They are traditionally made after the rice harvest, in the winter months, often at *Poush Sahkranti*, which is a phase of the moon during the month of *Poush* (December/January). This is one of many sweets made with new-season ground rice, and its name comes from *nonta* (salty) and *puli* (style of rice flour).

Makes about 15

3 medium sweet potatoes, boiled (about 20–30 minutes) and peeled

2½ tbsp rice flour

2 tbsp all-purpose flour

salt

vegetable oil

liquid jaggery (optional)

Filling

1 tbsp vegetable oil

1 cup shelled peas

2 tsp fennel seeds, finely ground

1½ tsp fresh ground black pepper

1 tsp sugar

a pinch of salt

1 It is important to drain the sweet potatoes thoroughly, and to let them dry out as they cool. Put them in a bowl, add the flours and a pinch of salt, and mash thoroughly until very smooth.

2 To make the filling, heat the 1 tbsp vegetable oil in a *karai* or heavy wok, and add all the remaining filling ingredients. Cook for 3–4 minutes, adding 1 tbsp water. Mash the peas. The taste should be a balance between sweet and savory.

3 Divide the potato mixture into 15 equal portions, and roll these into balls. Flatten 1 ball on the palm of your hand to a thick circle. Put 1 tsp of the pea filling to one side of the circle, and fold the edges over into a half-moon shape. Using your thumbs and forefingers, press the edges together to seal. Make another 14 cakes in the same way.

4 Heat the vegetable oil for deep-frying to medium, not hot, in a large shallow pan (like a paella pan). Arrange the cakes in the oil and let cook for about 20–25 minutes at a low heat. They will float to the surface as they cook, and so you should turn them around to color evenly.

5 Drain well and serve warm. You can drizzle them with liquid jaggery if you like.

Matar dal
Spiced lentils

This recipe was given to Simon Parkes by the gallery owner Supriya Banerjee. The dish is traditionally cooked to welcome the winter, using the first crop of winter vegetables such as green peas, *mooli*, and pumpkin (all of which grow on vines).

Serves 4

1¼ cups yellow split peas

salt

sugar

½ tsp turmeric

2 tbsp vegetable oil

2 dried bay leaves

2 medium potatoes, peeled and cubed

1 medium sweet potato, peeled and cubed

4 *patol* (wax or ivy gourds), scraped and cubed

1 cup pumpkin flesh, cubed

1 small *mooli* (white radish), peeled and cubed

1 cup sugar snap peas, strings removed and halved

5–6 young bottle gourd shoots (you could use zucchini flowers)

1½-inch piece fresh ginger, peeled and ground to a paste

4 medium fresh green chilis, cut lengthwise if you want heat or whole for flavor only

2 tbsp ghee

1 tsp panch phoran (*see* page 54)

1 Soak the split peas for 2 hours, then change the water and put them in warm water to cover in a medium saucepan. Bring to a boil, then simmer for 30 minutes. Add a pinch each of salt and sugar, and the turmeric.

2 Heat the vegetable oil in a *karai* or heavy wok, add the bay leaves and fry for 60 seconds. Then add the vegetables in sequence (as listed), at regular intervals, depending on how long they take to cook — the whole process should take about 20 minutes. When adding the sugar snap peas, add the ginger paste, the chilis, and split peas. Continue cooking until the vegetables are ready.

3 In a separate *karai* or heavy wok, melt the ghee and cook the panch phoran until the spices crackle. Pour this on top of the vegetables and dal mixture and stir well. Serve with boiled rice.

Khashundi Mustard sauce

Makes about 1 quart

6 cups water

1 tsp sugar

1 tsp turmeric

salt

1-inch piece fresh ginger, peeled and grated to a paste

2 medium unripe green mangoes, peeled and sliced

Seeds and spices

7 cups yellow mustard seeds

2 tsp cumin seeds

1 tsp onion seeds

seeds from 3 green cardamom pods

1-inch cinnamon stick

3 cloves

1 tsp fennel seeds

1 tbsp coriander seeds

¼ tsp fenugreek seeds

3 dried red chilis, torn and seeded

3 medium dried bay leaves

This sauce is usually made in the summer months to last throughout the year. It is one way of combining the flavor of green mangoes with the heat of mustard and a fine blend of spices. It's an excellent accompaniment to fried snacks and meals of vegetables and rice.

1 Put all the seeds and spices into a spice mill and grind to a very fine powder. (It would take much longer in a mortar and pestle.)

2 Bring the water to a boil in a large pan, reduce to a simmer, and gradually add the powdered spices, stirring briskly so no lumps form. Add the sugar, turmeric, salt to taste, and the ginger, and simmer steadily for about half an hour, or slightly longer, until reduced to about 1 quart in volume.

3 Remove from the heat and add the mango slices while it is still hot. Check for the salt-sugar balance. Cover and keep at room temperature for 24 hours. (In Bengal, we would leave it in the sun for a couple of days to mellow.)

4 Remove the mango and bottle the sauce in clean containers. (The mango can be used in cooking or in dals.)

Index

Bibliography

Achaya, K.T., *Indian Food: A Historical Companion*, Oxford University Press, 1994.

Banerjea, Dr Dhrubajyoti, *European Calcutta: Images and Recollections of a Bygone Era*, UBS Publishers' Distributors Pvt. Ltd, 2005.

Banerji, Chitrita, *The Hour of the Goddess*, Seagull Books, 2001.

Banerji, Chitrita, *Life and Food in Bengal*, Weidenfeld & Nicolson, 1991.

Brennan, Jennifer, *Curries and Bugles: A Cookbook of the British Raj*, Penguin, 1992.

Burton, David, *The Raj at Table*, Faber & Faber, 1993.

Busteed, H.E., *Echoes from Old Calcutta*, Rupa & Co., 1908.

Chaudhuri, Sukanta, ed., *Calcutta: The Living City — Volumes 1 and 2*, Oxford University Press, 1990.

Collingham, Lizzie, *Curry: A Biography*, Chatto & Windus, 2005.

DasGupta, Minakshie, *Bangla Ranna: The Bengal Cookbook*, UBS Publishers' Distributors Ltd, 1982.

DasGupta, Minakshie, Bunny Gupta and Jaya Chaliha, *The Calcutta Cook Book*, Penguin India, 1995.

David, Elizabeth, *Harvest of the Cold Months*, Michael Joseph, 1994.

Davidson, Alan, ed., *Penguin Companion to Food*, Penguin, 2002.

Davidson, Alan, ed., *The Wilder Shores of Gastronomy*, Ten Speed Press, 2002.

Gupta, R.P., *Fish and the Bengali* (Maachh Ar Bangali), Anandabazar, 1989.

Moorhouse, Geoffrey, *Calcutta: The City Revealed*, Weidenfeld & Nicolson, 1971.

O'Hagan, Andrew, ed., *The Weekenders: Adventures in Calcutta*, Ebury Press, 2004.

Panjabi, Camellia, ed., *The Taj Magazine. Calcutta*, The Taj Group of Hotels, 1989.

Richardson, Tim, *Sweets: A History of Temptation*, Bantam Press, 2002.

Roden, Claudia, *The Book of Jewish Food*, Viking, 1997.

Singh, Raghubir, *Calcutta: The Home and the Street*, Thames and Hudson, 1988.

Sinha, Anil Kishore, *Anthropology of Sweetmeats*, Gyan Publishing House, New Delhi, 2000.

Wright, Bob, ed., *Calcutta 200 Years. A Tollygunge Club Perspective.* Tollygunge Club Ltd, Calcutta, 1981.

Wyvern [pseud.], *Sweet Dishes: A Little Treatise*, Higginbottom & Co., Madras, 1881.

Authors' acknowledgements

Page 15: The quotation from *A Strange and Sublime Address* by Amit Chaudhuri, is printed by kind permission of Pan Macmillan.

The authors wish to thank the following for their generous assistance and support:

In Calcutta: Nondon Bagchi; Supriya Banerjee; Ranvir Bhandari at the Sheraton Sonar Bangla Hotel; Jaya Chaliha; Tamashru Chandra Chandra; Joydeep Chatterjee; Amit Chaudhuri; Ashok Das; Rakhi Dasgupta and the staff of Kewpie's Kitchen; Karuna Devi; George George at the Oberoi Grand Hotel; Dr. Dhrubajyoti Ghosh; Moni Gupta; Rupa Halim; Deepika Jaidka; Moina Jhala; Sonia John; Shaun Kenworthy; Nitin Shivji Kothari; Monica Liu; Pushie & Danny Mahtab; Anita & Samir Mukherjee; David Nahoum; Neil O'Brien; B.C. Ojha; Priya Paul; Afroze Randherian; Ankur Roy Chowdhury; Rakhi Sarkar; Aveek Sen; Paritosh Sen; Biswaranjan Sengupta; Violet Smith; the late Bob Wright O.B.E.; Anne Wright; and Ian Zachariah. Thanks too to the many cooks, street and market vendors who gave of their knowledge so freely.

In the U.K: Aroup Chatterjee; Sheila Dillon; Graham Ellis; Susan Fleming; The Guild of Food Writers (especially Clarissa Hyman and Michael Raffael); Gulf Air; Sir Anthony & Lady Hayward; Jason Lowe; Lawrence Morton; Jill Norman; Indar & Aruna Pasricha; Tony Phillips; David Prest; Prof. Tapan & Hashi Raychaudhuri; Amit Roy; Simon Scaddan; Atreyee Sen; Chandak Sengoopta; Dixi Stewart; and Rebecca Wells.

Finally, special thanks go to Rudrangshu Mukherjee and Rebecca Spry, whose support and encouragement and whose eye for detail has been unfailing throughout.

Publisher's acknowledgements

Thanks to Kamran at Multilingual Solutions Ltd, Ground Floor, 27 Stonar Road, London W14 8RZ for the Bengali script.